York St Jo...

Sports History

Sports History

A Practical Guide

Martin Polley

palgrave
macmillan

First published 2007 by
PALGRAVE MACMILLAN
Houndmills, Basingstoke, Hampshire RG21 6XS and
175 Fifth Avenue, New York, N.Y. 10010
Companies and representatives throughout the world

PALGRAVE MACMILLAN is the global academic imprint of the Palgrave Macmillan division of St. Martin's Press, LLC and of Palgrave Macmillan Ltd. Macmillan® is a registered trademark in the United States, United Kingdom and other countries. Palgrave is a registered trademark in the European Union and other countries.

ISBN-13: 978–1–4039–4074–2 hardback
ISBN-10: 1–4039–4074–6 hardback
ISBN-13: 978–1–4039–4075–9 paperback
ISBN-10: 1–4039–4075–4 paperback

This book is printed on paper suitable for recycling and made from fully managed and sustained forest sources.

A catalogue record for this book is available from the British Library.

A catalog record for this book is available from the Library of Congress.

10   9   8   7   6   5   4   3   2   1
16   15   14   13   12   11   10   09   08   07

Printed and bound in China

For Martin Wright

Contents

Acknowledgements

At Palgrave, thanks go to Terka Acton for her enthusiasm and support, and to Sonya Barker and Beverley Tarquini for their guidance in the final stages. Frank Galligan gave some helpful early advice on the project. My colleagues in the sports team at the University of Southampton have assisted me in various ways, with Julie Price and Candice Williams, in particular, helping to make a breathing space possible, and Anna Chivers providing crucial technical help. Thomas Huelin and Georgina Wright deserve special thanks for reading a number of the chapters in draft form and for providing constructive feedback. Martin Johnes and an anonymous reviewer read the whole text, and made many useful suggestions that have improved the book. Finally, I am grateful to my family for putting up with the disruption that books always bring, and for all the help and care they have given me. To James and Edward, and to Catherine, 'my beautiful comrade from the north', thank you.

The 1895 map of St Marylebone appears with the kind permission of the City of Westminster Archives Centre.

Introduction

One of the signs that an academic subject is growing in maturity and popularity is the publication of textbooks designed to help students develop their practical skills. The academic study of sport, now a regular feature in many universities' undergraduate and postgraduate programmes and well represented in schools and colleges, is no exception. New books, such as Chris Gratton and Ian Jones' social science-based *Research Methods for Sport Studies* and David Andrews, Daniel Mason, and Michael Silk's *Qualitative Methods in Sport Science*, have joined such perennials as Jerry Thomas and Jack Nelson's frequently revised *Research Methods in Physical Activity*.[1] Specialised methodologies also have their texts, such as Nikos Ntoumanis' guide to SPSS, and some thematic areas have also been covered, as in Gill Clarke and Barbara Humberstone's guide to *Researching Women and Sport*.[2] This diversity, which is also reflected in the growing methodology literature in the related areas of leisure, tourism, and hospitality, is indicative of sport's ever-widening scope as a discipline.[3] In educational institutions throughout the world, the academic study of sport has grown since the 1960s from being an adjunct to physical education into a fully-fledged discipline with its own degrees, professional support networks, publications, societies, and career paths.

In recognition of this growth, this book is designed to complement the growing methodology literature by adding another important specialised area into the mix: history. Historical approaches to sport are firmly embedded in the study of sport. For example, in the United Kingdom (UK), the Quality Assurance Agency's 2000 benchmark statement on what a sports-based degree should contain included the recognition of history's importance in its call for the study of the 'historical, social, political, economic diffusion, distribution and impact of sport'.[4] A-level courses (those taken by students at the age of 18) include sections on history, as in Edexcel's physical education (PE) course with its historical themes in units on 'The Social Basis of Sport and Recreation' and 'Global Trends in International Sport'.[5] History's presence in such programmes is a testimony to sports educationalists' assumption that if we wish to understand sport holistically, we have to study its past alongside all the other aspects – sociological, scientific, managerial, pedagogical, and so on – that make up a typical sports-based programme. While the proportion of time devoted to history varies from course to course, most sports students in further and higher education have to engage with history at some point in their studies.

This presence is both desirable and necessary. Not only does it give students – and thus many of the future personnel of the wide-ranging sports industry – a sense of perspective on the present condition of sport, it also helps them to gain analytical, research, and judgemental skills that can be useful in a variety of settings. Moreover, sports history can help students to develop a critical approach to sport. This can help them recognise the fact that sport is not simply natural, but is a cultural product linked to all kinds of contexts and traditions, and carrying both positive and negative values relative to those settings. Sports history, when practised well, can help students move beyond the common sense of current sport and give them the insight and vocabulary needed to explore such questions as what, how, when, where, and why. Sports history also shares the intellectual challenge common to all historical studies, and it is worthy of inclusion on sports programmes for its stimulating and provocative nature. However, it is clear from any analysis of the composition of sports courses that historical methodology is not, on the whole, taught in depth. Gratton and Jones' complaint in their invaluable methodology books that 'there are few specialist texts available for the sports researcher approaching the subject from the social sciences perspective'[6] can be amplified when we come to history. Douglas Booth's 2005 *The Field: Truth and Fiction in Sport History* has made an impact, offering as it does a sophisticated and enthusiastic critique of the ways in which sports historians work and the relationship between theory and practice in the discipline. Apart from this, the most significant contributions have been individual chapters in larger methodology books, such as Nancy Struna's chapter in Thomas, Nelson, and Silverman, and David Wiggins and Daniel Mason's chapter in Andrews, Mason, and Silk: but these apart, history tends to be marginal to the concerns of the authors of methodology textbooks.[7]

From another angle, there is no shortage of literature on historical methodology aimed at people studying history, ranging from such classics as E.H. Carr's *What is History?*, Geoffrey Elton's *The Practice of History*, and Arthur Marwick's *The Nature of History* through to Keith Jenkins' philosophical *Re-thinking History* and Jeremy Black and Donald MacRaild's hands-on *Studying History*.[8] However, this genre of literature rarely mentions sports history, and it is not marketed – either by its publishers or by teachers and lecturers – in a way that makes it accessible to sports students who are studying history. The low profile of practical and philosophical guidance on doing sports history is exacerbated by the fact that many sports students give history up at an early stage in their formal education, and thus enter sports degree programmes without any real grounding in what the study of history entails. The obstacles that this situation can cause can be illustrated through a comparison: imagine sports students without a good school-leaving qualification in biology attempting a degree-level sports physiology course. Broadly, sports students tend to prioritise the scientific, vocational, and practical sides of sport, and to develop their skills in areas other than history. This book is designed to help students develop their historical skills, to demystify history as a subject and make it more accessible to sports students, and to bridge the conceptual and methodological gaps that exist between history and the other disciplines on their courses.

However, this book is not aimed solely at sports students. Many history degree programmes now contain sports-based material. This book is designed to help history students taking sports history elements by providing historiographical, conceptual, and methodological guidance on their chosen area. It is also aimed at those history students who have so far not engaged with sports history, to give them some insights into this growth area. As we shall see in Chapter 3, the academic history establishment was indifferent towards sport for decades, and there has been a struggle to have sport's legitimacy as a subject worthy of study recognised. The influence of the historical sports sceptics is declining in the face of highly rated research in sports history, and in the growing recognition of sport's importance in past societies. In this time of disciplinary fluidity, this book is designed to get history students and their tutors thinking about sport, both as an area for original research and as a case study in applied historiography. The book is thus designed to help sports-based students work effectively as historians, and to help history students look at sport as a subject that can give them new insights to the periods and societies they are studying.

In order to deliver these aims, the book deals with ideas and practice in sports history, and aims to help you develop a sophisticated approach to the subject so that you can understand it, enjoy it, and practise it in a professional way. To get you started, this Introduction is followed by a section called 'Warm-Up Exercises', designed to get you thinking socially, critically, and historically about sport. Chapter 1 deals with the fundamental question of what history and sports history are, and why we should study them. These questions may seem to be basic, but unless you question the identity of your subject, you will never gain a good understanding of it. This chapter will also help you appreciate both the diversity of the subject matter and its contested nature. With working definitions in place, Chapter 2 will explore the ways in which the past is embedded in contemporary sport, and the implications that this inter-relationship has for us as sports historians. Sport is so tightly rooted in the past that it is simply not viable to ignore its history if we want to understand it. However, so much of sport's engagement with its past is conducted in mythologised or one-sided ways, and we need to appreciate this culture before we move on to study sports history academically. In Chapter 3, we will look at the growth of an academic interest in sports history, outlining the developments within the discipline of history that have made this exciting area of study possible, and looking at some of the ways in which these developments are still traceable in the preoccupations of sports history today. Chapter 4 then explores the different kinds of text that you are likely to use by providing a critical overview of the different genres of sports history. These chapters all use practical exercises to give you the opportunity to develop some of the skills needed for historical thinking.

From Chapter 5, the emphasis shifts to the primary materials of history itself. Chapter 5 introduces primary evidence and the issues that surround it, while Chapters 6 and 7 explore different types of evidence that sports historians use. By working through these sources, these three chapters will help you to develop the analytical tools needed to work as a historian, and they will encourage you to seek out your own historical evidence rather than just rely on the samples of primary sources provided in textbooks and class materials. Chapter 8 will then apply the book's strands into some concrete guidance on the kind of original sports history research project that you could carry out, before a brief Conclusion ties up some of the book's strands and highlights some of the issues in sports history that you need to remain engaged with in the future.

The book is designed to be read through continuously. In particular, you are encouraged to engage with the conceptual material so that you can move towards an understanding of what sports history is about before you attempt to practise it. The exercises and activities, which you can do alone or with others, are designed to help you make the ideas concrete, and to show how sports history is not just an academic study, but a living part of contemporary sports culture. In addition, a number of specialised words and phrases are defined in the Glossary at the end of the book.

▶ A note on further reading

All works cited and quoted in the text are referenced in each chapter's endnotes. The Further Reading section at the end of the book does not simply list all of these items. Instead, it focuses on some key texts in five kinds of reading that you need to do in conjunction with this book: large-scale histories of sport; historical theory and methodology; sports studies; sports history bibliographies; and journals. In addition, it provides a listing of some essential websites for sports historians.

Warm-Up Exercises

Before we move into the conceptual and practical guidance that this book is designed to deliver, I am going to put you through an intellectual warm-up routine. Just as you should always warm-up physically before taking part in any sport or exercise, so it is worth spending some time on a mental warm-up when tackling a new area. As will become clear later in the book, working as a sports historian is very different from working in other areas of sports studies, particularly those based on the sciences; and this chapter is designed to help you get yourself into an appropriate frame of mind with which to tackle sports history. Similarly, for history students who have not tackled sport as a subject matter before, these steps will help you set up sport as a legitimate area for intellectual enquiry. These exercises are particularly useful if you are a sports enthusiast who has not approached sport academically before, as they will help you to move beyond a common sense acceptance of sport and into a more enquiring position.

The warm-up steps here are all based on some basic assumptions that you need to recognise when approaching sport historically. These assumptions may well be of second nature to you already, or they may be new: either way, you need to engage with them. They are,

   Sport is not socially, politically, economically, culturally, or historic-
      ally neutral. Sport is always linked to the wider settings in which
      it is played, and to think that it can float free of them – as in, for
      example, the claim that 'sport and politics should not mix' – is an
      obstacle to your understanding of sport.
   Sport has both positive and negative features, and to concentrate only
      on the former and see sport without reservations as a force for good
      is to wilfully misunderstand it.
   If you want to understand sport, you have to be prepared to ask
      awkward questions of it, and to deal with any answers that may
      make you feel uncomfortable.
   Sport is just as much a legitimate area for historical study as war, reli-
      gion, social conditions, politics, and any other subject traditionally
      taught in history departments.

History is just as much a legitimate area for sports studies as physiology, psychology, pedagogy, sociology, management, and any other subject traditionally taught in sport departments.

You need to keep these assumptions in mind when using this book, as they underpin it. For now, let us move into the warm-up exercises.

▶ Exercise 1: Positive and negative sides to sport

It is easy for us as enthusiasts of sport – players, followers, coaches, officials, or whatever – to think only positively about it. We can easily recognise such positive aspects of sport as health promotion, socialisation, community building, and identity formation. However, it is sometimes harder to recognise sport's negative features that are the downsides to all of the positives. Below, I have given a number of everyday statements that emphasise the positive face of sport: 'Sport promotes health and well-being', 'Sport creates social mobility', and so on. I have then given a brief illustration of the kind of evidence that can be used to back up the positive statements, followed by a similarly brief illustration of the kind of evidence we could use to prove the opposite case. Your warm-up exercise is to find real evidence to back up each of the illustrations, the positive and the negative. This evidence can come from any historical period or place, or from your own experience and observation of real sport. I have given examples of all of the points to get you started. The point of the exercise is to get you recognising the ups and downs of sport, and appreciating the relationships between them.

Statement 1. Sport promotes health and well-being

Positive: Doctors recommend regular exercise as a preventative step against a wide range of conditions, including obesity, heart disease, depression, and osteoporosis.

Example: In 2004, the British government's Department of Health, in partnership with the Countryside Agency and Sport England, started a £2.6 million project to set up LEAPs – Local Exercise Action Pilots – in various communities. Each LEAP promotes and facilitates exercise and activity for targeted populations, such as diabetes sufferers and people recovering from strokes, as a specific way of improving health.

Negative: Sport causes injuries, ranging from mild sprains and grazes through to serious trauma to limbs, necks, heads, and chests. It can also cause death.

Example: Since the 1930s, at least six British fell-runners have died of hypothermia during competition after getting lost or falling in bad weather conditions.[1]

Statement 2. Sport creates social mobility

Positive: Successful sportsmen and women are able to move up the social scale and gain material success.

Example: British boxer Frank Bruno was brought up in a working-class community. He later claimed that sport helped him 'escape the poverty trap. Thanks to the rewards from boxing I am able to offer my wife and daughters a far better future than they could ever have hoped for had I still been stuck as a labourer on a building site.'[2]

Negative: For every sporting millionaire, there are thousands of also-rans who fail to achieve their sporting dreams, and have few qualifications or skills for other forms of work; and there are also many who are unable to handle the pressures that wealth and fame bring, and who succumb to various escapes – gambling, alcoholism and other substance abuse – that drain both their wealth and health. Social mobility in sport is unevenly distributed and easy to lose, and it can come at a price.

Example: George Best, a glamorous and talented Northern Irish footballer of the 1960s and 1970s, explained his rise and fall from player to pop icon to bankrupt alcoholic thus: 'I spent a lot of money on booze, birds and fast cars. The rest I just squandered.'[3] This famous piece of bravado fails to disguise a serious problem. Best died in 2005 at the age of 59 as a direct result of his alcohol abuse.

Statement 3. Sport brings communities together

Positive: Sport's links to geopolitical units – towns, cities, and countries – make it an ideal focus for the idea of community representation, and people who may not otherwise have anything in common with each other can find a shared interest in sport.

Example: When South Africa won the rugby union World Cup in 1995, in the immediate aftermath of the divisive apartheid years, the trophy was awarded to the team's Afrikaner captain Francois Pienaar by President Nelson Mandela, an icon of the black opposition to minority white rule. The presentation is described on a South African government website as 'a spontaneous gesture of racial reconciliation that melted hearts around the country. A single moment, and 400 years of colonial strife and bitterness... suddenly seemed so petty.'[4]

Negative: Sport's competitive nature and often aggressive character makes it just as suitable for expressing division as for promoting unity.

Example: In the Scottish city of Glasgow, the two leading football teams are strongly linked to two religious communities: Rangers to the Protestants and Celtic to the Roman Catholics. Despite some recent dilution of the sectarianism that has historically characterised these two clubs' cultures, the teams remain a focus for expressions of political, social, cultural, and religious differences within the city and beyond.

Statement 4. Sport makes people aspire towards excellence

Positive: Most people taking part in sport at any level will set themselves goals, ranging from winning an Olympic gold medal through to weight loss or simply beating a personal best. These goals inspire participants to commit themselves to their sport and abide by its laws and spirit.

Example: Rower Steve Redgrave won gold medals at five consecutive Olympic Games, from 1984 to 2000, as well as numerous other international competitions. An enthusiastic promoter of sport and exercise, a diabetic who has excelled despite his condition, an active charity fund-raiser, Redgrave is a model of sporting and personal excellence.

Negative: The pressure to succeed that is embedded in most sports' cultures, and the rewards – financial, personal, political – that can go with sporting success, mean that many people are willing to cheat in order to win. Excellence at any price is not excellence at all.

Example: In 1988, Canadian sprinter Ben Johnson won the men's 100 metres in the Seoul Olympic Games. In a post-race test, he was found to have been using the banned steroid stanozolol, and was disqualified and subsequently banned from athletics.

Statement 5. Sport helps people to socialise

Positive: Sport is an excellent way in which people of all ages, but particularly children, can meet new people and develop social skills – such as communication, taking turns, following rules, making decisions, and adopting leadership roles – that are useful in other areas of life. Sport can enhance confidence and self-esteem.

Example: Employers in the private and the public sector routinely use sports-based activities for staff development and team-building purposes.

Negative: For every child who enjoys sport, there is one who does not. Poor motor skills, uncorrected eyesight, disability, or a simple lack of interest leave many people alienated by compulsory sport at school, and can contribute to feelings of low self-esteem.

Example: Julie Myerson's moving childhood memoir, *Not a Games Person*, captures the feelings of isolation, alienation, and fear that can be caused by school sport and physical education. Her personal account is resonant for anyone who has ever felt this way: 'The swimming pool changing rooms are dark, damp and echoey. Lucky girls have letters about periods and verrucas...Everyone else stands and shivers in a miserable way, feet cold on the wet tiles, as they wait for Mrs Rogers to blow her whistle...If you don't dive in you'll be pushed from behind.'[5]

Working through these statements, and finding your own examples, is a good way to get you thinking critically about sport. Without such critical thinking, your engagement with sports history is likely to be limited. With it, you will be prepared to deal with the realities of sport rather than just its idealised image.

▶ Exercise 2: Putting sport in context

All sports take place in a context. This is a truism that you will find mentioned in most books on sports history and sports sociology, but its familiarity does not mean that you can take it for granted or ignore it. We will be exploring issues of context later on: for now, you need to do a simple exercise designed to help you identify the links between a sport's structure and nature and the wider societal setting in which it takes place.

Quidditch is a fictional sport invented by J.K. Rowling for her Harry Potter novels. It takes place in a magical community, based around schools of wizardry and witchcraft. The rules are explained in the first novel, *Harry Potter and the Philosopher's Stone*, and expanded in the charity spin-off, *Quidditch Through the Ages*.[6] It is a team invasion game played on flying broomsticks, involving different classes of balls that can act magically on their own volition. This sport is, obviously, a fantasy; yet the links between the context – in this case, a hidden world of witches and wizards, and that community's private school equivalents – and Quidditch's structure and nature are explicit. For this exercise, read the books named above, or watch the Quidditch sequences in the films of *Harry Potter and the Philosopher's Stone* and *Harry Potter and the Chamber of Secrets*, and make a list of all the features of the sport that position it as one that could happen only in that context. When we move on to deal with real sports later on, this exercise will have helped you tune your mind to making links between sport and context.

▶ Exercise 3: Empathy

Empathy is the act of identifying with other people's feelings and points of view. There has been a lot of discussion in history teaching circles about the role of empathy in historical study. The supporters of empathy argue that if we want to understand the past, we need to empathise with the people who lived then. This will help us understand the options that people felt they had, and their motivations for acting as they did. Opponents of empathy argue that it is impossible to empathise, as we cannot recreate past living, intellectual, and emotional conditions accurately enough to get into people's minds.[7] The sources that we have from the past – as will be discussed in Chapter 5 – are too incomplete and subjective for us to reconstruct people's ways of seeing the world and rationalising their behaviour. It is also difficult for us to attempt empathy with people whose beliefs, politics, and actions we find abhorrent. Imagine, for a moment, being asked to empathise historically with a slave-trader, a *Schutzstaffel* (SS) officer, or Joseph Stalin. However, despite its intellectual and ideological challenges, empathy is a useful quality for a historian to keep in mind, and you can warm-up for sports history by trying to apply it. It can help you appreciate opportunities, constraints, choices, and behaviour, and how all of these vary from time to time and place to place. How might you feel about sport if you had the wages, living conditions, and life expectancy of a thirteenth-century peasant? Why did a sportive culture based on the regular killing of people and animals, such as ancient Roman gladiatorial events, make sense to the people involved in it but seem repulsive to us? Why was religion central to the original Olympics Games but marginal to the modern Olympics? These are all huge questions that cannot be answered by empathy alone, but thinking through the mental world of the people involved, and the wider settings in which they lived, will help you approach the history, and might stop you making anachronistic judgements about sport in the past.

The exercise to help you develop this skill is based not on history, but on your own sporting life. Whoever you are, your own involvement in sport – which may range from elite performer to the kind of alienation cited in Julie Myerson's book above – will have been personal, but it will also have been influenced by such factors as your age, your gender, your social background, your income (or that of your family), where you live, the school you attended, your ethnicity, your ability, your religion, and many other factors. Some of these may seem irrelevant to you – if you are not religious, for example, you may fail to consider the relationship between faith and sport. However, all of these factors can have an influence on our individual sporting lives. Now put yourself in someone else's position, and try to imagine what his or her experiences of sport may be like. Work through the following scenarios:

- Imagine changing sex. Would you face discrimination or stereotyping in any sport? Would your opportunities to be involved in sport increase or decrease?
- Imagine changing ethnic group. Would your sporting experience change at all in relation to discrimination and opportunity?
- What would your sporting options be like if you were 30 years older than you are now? How about ten years younger?
- If you are a member of a faith that places restrictions on physical activity on certain days, how different might your sporting life be if you did not hold those obligations? If you are not part of such a faith, or you hold no religious beliefs, imagine taking on such observances. How would this affect your sporting participation?
- Imagine your personal income increasing by 50 per cent. What sporting opportunities could this open up to you? Now imagine your income decreasing by 50 per cent. What effect would this have on your sporting life?

To get a sense of these different positions, talk to people from the groups identified, and look at newspaper coverage and club and community websites to see what different sporting cultures are like. Not only will this give you a generally wide appreciation of the diversity of contemporary sport, it will also give you experience in attempting empathy, which will help your approaches to sports history.

▶ Exercise 4: Keeping your eyes and ears open

In Chapters 5, 6, and 7, we shall explore the diverse range of sources that you should use in your work on sports history. Before that, it is worth pausing to reflect on the ways in which sports history is embedded in the fabric of our communities. The skill to develop here is that of keeping your eyes and ears open to evidence about what sport was like in the past. Look for sports history in your local sports clubs' buildings, in street names (such as Archery Lane, Bowling Green Alley, Golf Course Road), and in the statues and memorials in your community.[8] Listen for sports history in older people's conversations: what do they mean when they compare a current player to a star from their younger days, or when they complain about declining standards in sport? To what are people alluding when they use idioms from the history of sport in everyday speech, such as 'Say it ain't so, Joe' or 'The best in the Northern Union'? Look for evidence of changing usage in a sports site. Why, for example, is the space that was built as a squash court in your local sports centre in the 1980s now a weights room or a children's play area? Why is there a derelict Victorian swimming pool in your town? Once you get into the habit of looking and listening for sports history in everyday life, you will increasingly appreciate the importance of the past in contemporary sport, a theme that we will develop in Chapter 2.

To warm-up in this area, do the following activities.

1. Using a map of your community, or of a large community near your home, find a road that has a sporting name. Contact the local authority to find out when it was given that name, and use old maps to see what was there before. Visit the area to see if there is any evidence of a continued sports usage.
2. Ask a member of your family from at least the generation above you to talk about what sport was like when he or she was the age that you are now, and to compare it to sport now. You might want to stick with one sport, or to open it up more broadly. Every time your interviewee names a person or a place that you do not know about, ask him or her to explain. End the interview by asking if sport was better then than it is now, and get reasons for this.

▶ Conclusion

These activities have been designed to help you warm-up for sports history. They have introduced some of the types of questioning you will need to do as a historian, and have given you the chance to explore your own examples, including unique ones from your own family and community history. Keep the skills here in mind as you move into the book, and as you begin your practical experience as a sports historian.

1 What is Sports History?

Asking such a basic question as 'What is sports history?' may seem to be too obvious a place to start. Common sense tells us what it must be: what happened in sport in the past. However, no historian of any subject ever got far by taking definitions only at the level of common sense; and the wider study of history is crowded with books and courses that attempt to define the discipline's terms of engagement. In his excellent survey of some of the philosophical issues raised by studying history, *History: What and Why?*, Beverley Southgate quotes Plato's dictum that 'The life which is unexamined is not worth living', and applies this view to the study of history:

> it is arguable that 'unexamined history' ... is not worth doing ... [W]e need, as historians no less than as human beings, some self-awareness, some understanding of what it is we are trying to do, and of why we are trying to do it.[1]

This approach is taken as the starting point for this chapter. It is based on two assumptions: first, that you will understand sports history more fully if you spend some time reflecting on its nature than if you rely on common sense alone; and second, that your work as a sports historian will be most effective if it is based on some engagement with a wider sense of history's character and purpose. The chapter aims to introduce you to these issues, first by looking broadly at the nature of history, and then by characterising sports history itself. For history students new to sport as a subject matter, this chapter will consolidate your appreciation of the 'What is history?' debate, and introduce you to the contours of sports history. This survey can only be introductory, and you should follow up and read out from the references to go into this subject in depth.

▶ 1.1 What is history?

If you are a student of history, then it is likely that you will already be familiar with this question. If you are coming to sports history from a sports studies or sports science background, then it will probably be a new one. Either way, it is a crucial one for you to address, as it will give you a conceptual foundation for your studies in sports history. Reflecting on the nature of the discipline, in the manner advocated by Southgate above, can help you rationalise what you do in your sports history, and make connections between sports history and other things that people have done in the past.

There is a huge literature devoted to the question of history's nature and identity. Probably, the most important point we can make in this brief survey is that history's nature is disputed and debated between historians. Jeremy Black and Donald MacRaild refer to 'the shifting and often confusing grounds of historical inquiry',[2] and you need to recognise at this early stage in your sports history work that the grounds do shift. The terms of the debate are often accessed by history students through two influential books from the 1960s: E.H. Carr's philosophical *What is History?*, first published in 1961; and Geoffrey Elton's more practical *The Practice of History* of 1967. However, these two were not the first or last word in the debate, and there are many other texts that you should use to guide your way in this fascinating subject. Arthur Marwick's *The Nature of History*, Beverley Southgate's *History: What and Why?*, John Tosh's *The Pursuit of History*, and Black and MacRaild's accessible *Studying History* all provide a blend of debate, practical guidance, and examples which will help you navigate those 'shifting and often confusing grounds'.[3] For our current purposes, we are going to consider seven snapshots about the nature of history. If you want to work successfully as a sports historian, then it is worth your while to reflect on these snapshots.

1.1.1 The multiple meanings of the word 'history'

'History' means a number of different things. Its common sense meaning is 'the past': history is what has happened, and where we have come from. Next, it can mean a narrative, close to the French setting where *histoire* covers both 'history' and 'story'. We use it in this sense to refer to the story of a particular event, or related series of events, such as 'The history of the Second World War' or, in a sporting setting, 'The history of baseball'. A third meaning is more about the present: history is what historians write, and is thus different from the past. History here is thus made by historians. Finally, we can see history – often with a capital H – as being a structured academic discipline, similar to Physics, Geography, or Biology, with its own courses, university departments, and networks. This is history as a profession and a discipline. Some of these meanings are at odds with others: in particular, it can be difficult to see history both as what happened in the past and as something that historians create in the present. The point here is to help you tune in to the different meanings of the word that will come up in your reading, and to guide you in using the meaning appropriate to the context in your own work.

1.1.2 Positivism and relativism

Different historians approach their subject from different philosophical positions. The two main areas are often called positivism and relativism. A positivist approach to the past is one which assumes that the truth of what happened in the past can be discovered. Here, it is the historian's job to locate, sift, and analyse the evidence from the time, and to establish what happened and why. The well-trained historian is seen, in this tradition, as an objective reporter and analyst, or as a detective attempting to bring the evidence together to work out what happened. This approach is related to positivist traditions in science, which assume that the truth is discoverable through carefully designed experimentation and observation. Historians writing from relativist positions, however, view the notion of 'historical truth' as problematic due to the incomplete and subjective nature of the evidence itself. Moreover, they draw attention to the historian's own position in writing history, and argue that the historian's own biography – his or her gender, social class, nationality, religion, and political affiliations, for example – will all have a subjective effect on what gets written. This tradition also emphasises the relationship between the time and the place in which the historian is working and the aspects of history that he or she studies. We shall return to these positions later in this book in relation to sports history: for now, it is important for you to be aware of the basic positions and start thinking about your own views on them.

1.1.3 The importance of evidence

Although the two positions outlined above have different approaches to evidence, all historians are agreed on the basic point that unless there is some evidence from the past, there can be no historical study. There are many types of evidence, such as documentary, archaeological, artistic, linguistic, cultural, geographical, and architectural: we shall explore these later in this book in relation to sports history in Chapters 5, 6, and 7. Whatever the type, the importance of evidence is hard to challenge: without some kind of source material from the past, we as historians cannot begin to know what happened. Recognition of this situation is fundamental at this stage. An appreciation of the nature and significance of what historians call 'primary sources' will help you read sports history books with sensitivity, and will help you in making your own choices about what aspects of the past to study. Put simply, there is no point in you committing to a study of an aspect of sports history for which no evidence has survived; and conversely, you need to consider carefully taking on a subject with an abundance of sources. Either way, the bottom line is clear: no evidence, no history.

1.1.4 History is political

Whatever happened in the past has gone. We may be living with its aftermath, but there is nothing that we can do to change it. However, an important aspect of the nature of history that you need to recognise now is that we – as individuals and as communities – constantly rewrite the past in the light of our current needs and interests. Think personally for a moment of how you may relate an incident from your childhood in a way that makes you appear in a positive light. Think socially about how communities will look at past events in the light of contemporary needs, as in such public aspects of history as which figures have statues put up to them and which parts of the past are taught in schools. History here is thus about conflict and power, as different groups within society – say, different religious communities or ethnic groups – will struggle with each other about how history should be seen: think, for example, of the debates that have surrounded the British recognition of Holocaust Memorial Day, or the discussions over governments apologising for things that happened centuries ago, such as slavery, colonisation, or genocide. This is not a recent development, and it would be naïve to ascribe it to 'political correctness': political and ideological influences have always characterised people's dealings with the past, and naming a street after a Boer War battle in the 1900s was just as much a political act as renaming it after Nelson Mandela in the 1980s. This ties in strongly with the relativists' assumptions outlined above: the history we get is relative to the time and the place from which we are looking.

1.1.5 History is about debates

You will already be aware that there is some debate about the nature of history itself. Within the discipline, debating is also a key feature of research and writing. In all areas, the work of one historian will typically be challenged by another historian, and debates will develop over particular themes. These debates focus on many different aspects of the past: the causes of wars, the standard of living, the significance of a particular person or movement, or the reasons for a particular occurrence. Debates happen when historians from different positions, or writing at different times, look at the evidence in a way that leads them to argue against their predecessors' findings. Once you are aware of this, you will be able to read the literature effectively, and you will be able to recognise different themes running through different books and articles. This awareness will also help you to recognise that no history book is ever the final word on a subject: there will always be a chance for someone else to come at the subject again from another angle to challenge our existing views. It also shows how studying history is not just about learning dates, but is about analysis, interpretation, and dialogue.

1.1.6 History is specialised

While history as a subject may be debated, history as an academic discipline has some fairly clear structures. From school curricula through to university departments, history has a presence within the academic life of all countries, complete with its professional networks of conferences, learned societies, journals, publishers, museums, libraries, and archives. Moreover, history as a subject is divided into various categories, known as sub-disciplines. The largest of these vary across time, evidence of the point made above about history being about what the present wants from the past. For example, ecclesiastical and constitutional history were major areas for historians working in the nineteenth century, but, as tastes and contemporary requirements have altered, they have been eclipsed by social and cultural history. At present, it is easy to identify political history, social history, economic history, and cultural history as the most obvious umbrella sub-disciplines. This division may seem arbitrary, and there is often enormous overlap between areas. For example, it is impossible to write social history effectively without taking account of political, economic, and cultural factors, so boundaries between sub-disciplines are softer and more permeable than they may first appear. At the same time, history as a discipline is increasingly outward looking, with historians and academics in other fields – such as archaeology, anthropology, geography, political sciences, and cultural studies – creating interrelationships that can increase our knowledge and understanding of the past.

1.1.7 Our history was other people's present

Finally, it is worth stepping back from the discipline and its attendant debates to remember that what we call 'history' or 'the past' was the present for other people. An appreciation of this simple fact is useful when faced with debates about the nature of history. The people who lived through what we are studying were not thinking of themselves in the historical terms that we use for them, but were simply getting on with their lives: fighting their wars, having their families, worshipping their gods, working in their fields, or whatever. Keep this in mind whenever you come across historians using shorthand terms such as 'between the wars' or 'before the industrial revolution', and remember that the people who lived then could not have known what they were between or before. The period we now call 'medieval' or 'the middle ages' was, for the people living through it, nothing to do with the middle of anything: to them, each day was the present. Remembering this can also help you to avoid anachronistic judgements about past people's behaviour, beliefs, or motives. Burning women accused of witchcraft, voting for a dictator, or basing an entire economy on a single crop may all strike us as foolish things for people in the past to have done: but those acts must have made sense or been viable options for the people who did them, and to criticise them only in the light of later evidence or opinions does not make for good history.

These seven snapshots cover a huge amount of ground. For now, they should have given you a sense of the issues at stake, and should have moved you on from uncritically accepting that 'history' simply means 'the past'. Read around these themes to get proper insights to the key question, 'What is history?'

Activity 1: Moving towards a definition of history

The themes covered above should have shown you that history is not easy to define. However, unless you reflect on your own attitude towards history, and try to position yourself in the debate, any sports history you do will be based on weak intellectual foundations. Below are four quotations from different historians, about the nature and identity of history. Read all of them — ideally, go to the originals and read around the quotations, too, so that you can see the assumptions and evidence that helped shape each author's view — and then answer the questions below:

Quotations

(a) '[History is the] actions of human beings that have been done in the past'. R.G. Collingwood, 1946.[4]

(b) 'History is a continuous process of interaction between the historian and his facts, an unending dialogue between the past and the present'. E.H. Carr, 1961.[5]

(c) 'The study of history amounts to a search for the truth'. Geoffrey Elton, 1967.[6]

(d) 'History is not "the past", nor yet the surviving past. It is a reconstruction of certain parts of the past (from surviving evidence) which in some way have had relevance for the present circumstances of the historian who reconstructed them.' Gordon Connell-Smith and Howell A. Lloyd, 1972.[7]

Questions

1. Which of the quotations most closely resembles your view of history? Why?

2. With which of the quotations do you most strongly disagree? Why?

3. Once you have done this, write your own single sentence answer to the question 'What is history?'

▶ 1.2 What is sports history?

Sports history may be easier to define than history as a whole; but once again, there are various activities that could be given the name. For our purposes, we can identify three distinct but overlapping answers.

Type 1 sports history is everything that happened in the past relating to sport. This is the day-to-day, year-to-year real-time events that people who lived in the past did whenever they played games. Much of it has left no evidence behind, just as much of your own day-to-day sport leaves no traces. However, enough evidence has come to us – archaeological, literary, physical, visual, and in people's memories – for us to know that sports, physical exercises, and games have happened throughout human history.

Type 2 sports history is the narrative of those events. This is the act of looking back on the past of sport through the evidence that we do have, and telling its story. This is the kind of approach that Richard Holt has characterised with his biblical comparison as 'little more than the book of Chronicles or the book of Numbers'.[8] This kind of history, which often focuses on a specific club, provides us with chronologies of events, and with details and anecdotes about players, teams, and competitions. We shall examine this kind of history writing in Chapter 3. For now, we can simply note it as a type of sports history, a type usually classified as 'popular' or 'non-academic', and one characterised by what Booth calls a 'reconstructionist' approach, where historians go to the primary sources and attempt to simply narrate the story of what happened.[9]

Type 3 sports history is the contextual analysis of those events. This answer to the question 'What is sports history?' is the one with which academic historians would feel most comfortable, as they see their role as being the detailed exploration of what sport was like in the past in relation to the society in which it was taking place. It is an outward-looking definition, one that sees sport as being interrelated with social, political, religious, economic, and cultural trends. It is an approach that finds something lacking in the popular sports history characterised above, and would find resonance in W.G. Hoskins' criticism of popular local history for being 'preoccupied with facts and correspondingly unaware of problems'.[10] This type of sports history goes beyond the facts and into the problems, and is characterised by J.A. Mangan's aim to 'set sport in its full cultural context', with attention paid to 'sequence, tendencies, outcomes and change'.[11] Booth's 'constructionist' and, to a certain extent, 'deconstructionist' historians fit into this type of sports history: although they differ on many matters, both types are interested in going beyond face value of facts and narratives, and in analysing sport's past.[12] This is the type of sports history towards which you should aspire.

A quick example using a real sporting event can illustrate these three answers, and show us how the different meanings of sports history typified above are interrelated. The Ashes is the trophy competed for in cricket test matches between England and Australia. A type 1 sports history is the series of events that have taken place from the 1880s onwards in the contests between the two countries' teams, the day-to-day acts of players, administrators, and spectators in their own present. A type 2 sports history is the detailed record of the Ashes that you could construct from the primary sources such as newspapers, cricket almanacs, and players' memoirs. This would be a ball-by-ball, match-by-match, and series-by-series narrative of this particular rivalry. A type 3 sports history would be an analysis of the Ashes phenomenon in such wider contexts as cricket's development and diffusion, imperial and Commonwealth relations, English and Australian models of national identity and masculinity, and sporting and media technology.

Activity 2: Past – narrative – analysis

Using the model of the Ashes given above, you now need to develop your own example of the three levels of sports history. Family history is a useful way into this, due to its accessibility and its unique nature for you.

1. Talk to an older member of your family about his or her sporting interests when he or she was younger, trying to focus in on a particular period — say, a season in which he or she played for a school team, or a time when he or she attended a major sporting event. Identify any evidence that might survive from this time, such as photographs, newspapers, diaries, letters, and artefacts. This will give you a sense of the first level discussed above: sports history as what happened in the past.

2. Try to construct a chronological narrative of the events you have uncovered. Be as accurate as you can with dates, and try to be as objective as possible in the way you list the items. The aim is to produce a reliable and trustworthy chronicle of the time. This will give you some experience of the second level: sports history as a narrative.

3. With the narrative in place, try to step back and start asking analytical questions that can help you place the sporting events in context. What links are there between your family member's gender and the sport in

---

question? How much would the sport have cost (both financially and in terms of time), and what does this tell you about the links between sport, income, and social class? Was the sport in question representative of a community, such as a school, a village, or a city? If so, what kind of image did the sport give of that community? These are just examples of the kind of questions you can ask here. Using a conceptual map or a spider diagram, make as many links as you can between the sporting events in your family member's past and the time and the place in which they happened. This will give you a sense of the third level: sports history as an analytical study of what happened.

There are thus different answers to the question 'What is sports history?', and the different answers relate both to the past itself – the historical events – and to the ways in which people in the present approach them. This diversity is not a reason to avoid sports history: indeed, the debates that arise out of the different approaches are part of sports history's intellectual appeal. Sports history, then, is far more than just a part of your syllabus, or an optional area that you might like to study for a project. It is a dynamic sub-discipline of history, one that connects with many other areas of historical study. Moreover, history is more than just a background for the socio-historical parts of a sports studies course. It is a stimulating and philosophically challenging discipline concerned with the human past in all its varieties. However, 'what is . . . ' definitions can take us only so far: for any deeper understanding of history as a whole and sports history in particular, we need to move on to the question of 'why?'

▶ 1.3 Why study history?

Just as there is no simple answer to the question of history's identity, so there is no single rationale for the study of history. Every historian will have a different reason, and every official sanctioning of history – such as history as part of a state school curriculum – will be rationalised in terms of that state's own needs. However, as with our discussion of what history and sports history are, the absence of a single answer as to why we study history should not put us off asking the question. History is a popular academic subject throughout the world, despite its lack of obvious vocational application. It is also growing in popularity outside universities and schools through the proliferation of museums, heritage sites, television and radio documentaries, feature films and stage plays, the internet, romantic fiction, and community history projects. Why are so many people interested in knowing about the past? By examining some of the reasons, you can get your own approach to history in general and sports history in particular into focus.

First, knowing about the past can give people – as individuals and as members of communities – a sense of belonging and identity. Mobility and migration are typical features of modern societies. As people become more mobile, families more extended, and communities more ethnically and culturally diverse, it is natural that people should want to know something of their past. History – particularly family and community history – is about such roots. This interest is also evident at national level, with collective notions of history enshrined in the celebration of key dates from the past as holidays and times for reflection: Armistice Day in the UK, Independence Day and Martin Luther King's birthday in the United States of America (USA), Canada Day, Australia Day, and St Patrick's Day are all examples of this. Such events help to define a modern nation's shared history, and to keep the links between past and present alive. This can, of course, be problematic for multicultural nations, as the choice of which historical events to celebrate is an exercise in power and, inevitably, exclusion: the debate over establishing Martin Luther King Day in the USA and the ongoing controversies surrounding Holocaust Day in the UK are examples of this. The point remains, however, that history here is approached because it tells us something – maybe something very selective, but at least something – about where we have come from.

A second reason why we study history is that it can – ostensibly, at least – teach us lessons for the present and the future. One of the great clichés of history is that we should study it so that we can learn from past mistakes. This is not a view that stands up to much scrutiny: the wars, arms races, genocides, and famines that have taken place since the 1930s do not suggest that much was learnt from millennia of human experience. However, we can be more optimistic at the personal level, where we often act in ways informed by past situations. Organisations also do this, basing present decisions on past examples as well as projections about the future. It is important not to overplay this aspect of the past's appeal: but, at one level, we can see that we study history in order to compare present situations to past ones.

Third, history is popular because of its value in explaining the physical environments in which we find ourselves. Local and community history and archaeology are thriving, through academic coverage, adult education, field clubs, and local history societies. Wherever we live, the diverse nature of our townscapes and landscapes needs explanation, and only the historical and archaeological exploration of place can tell us about different building types and land-use patterns, and the timing of any community's growth or decline. Without historical awareness, the spaces in which we live, work, worship, and play can appear only as a random jumble of clashing layers. Imagine attempting to understand the different court markings on a multi-use sports hall's floor without any knowledge of each sport's laws: that is how baffling it is to look at a townscape or landscape without historical awareness. People study history because it helps them to make sense of their everyday surroundings. The same point can be made about the social settings in which we find ourselves. Knowledge of history helps us to make sense of such diverse aspects of our everyday lives as our political systems, the economic activities and forms of religion available to us, and the manners and protocols expected of us. We do not need to be reductionist, and claim that history explains everything: but it is clear that none of our systems were invented this morning, and that all have some form of inheritance from the past.

Taking these three brief reasons together, it is clear that the past matters to the present: as a place from which we came, a place from which we can learn, and a place which explains our current environments. The fact that history matters is the basic reason why it should be studied. If we leave the past unexamined, and simply live with its remnants – physical, social, mental – as so many myths that we accept without reflection, then we will be unable to make sense of our present. History gives us insight, perspective, and the ability to compare and contrast.

Activity 3: To study or not to study. . .

Using the themes covered above, take a piece of paper and mark out two columns. Head the left-hand column with the question 'Why should I study history?', and the right-hand column with the opposing question 'Why should I not study history?' Under each heading, write as many answers as you can think of. Make your answers as personal as possible, as this will help you reflect on your own attitudes towards history and your own strengths and weaknesses in approaching it.

If these are the basic reasons for studying history, then what case can be made for studying sports history? What is there about sport that makes its past worthy of the time, effort, and financial resources that sports historians devote to their work? The obvious answer is that we should study it because it happened. People played sports in the past, and these activities deserve to be studied just as much as those same people's religious habits, political systems, wars, or any other activities that take historians' attention. However, there is more to it than that. Sport is a cultural activity that is obsessed with the past, as witness the observance of traditions, the veneration of sites, and the obsession with records that permeate modern sport. Considering this aspect of sport can help us to appreciate its past not just as a subject that deserves to be studied, but as a living part of our everyday culture. The next chapter will explore this presence of the past in sport.

2 The Presence of the Past in Contemporary Sport

This book is a practical guide. It is designed to help you develop your understanding of sports history, and to improve your academic skills in this area. This chapter is dedicated to the first of these aspects – deepening your understanding. If you approach sports history simply as a part of your syllabus, and see it only as an academic subject, then you will miss out on a significant part of the interrelationship between sport and history. If, on the other hand, you step back and look at the ways in which the past permeates contemporary sports culture, then you will be able to see history as a meaningful component of everyday life, and not just as something dead with which historians deal.

Let us begin with a few snapshots taken between 2004 and 2006 that serve to illustrate some of the ways in which sport's past is engrained in its present.

- Soft drink manufacturer Coca-Cola sponsored the torch relay for the 2004 Olympic Games, stressing the historical nature of its commercial relationship with Olympism: 'As the Olympic Movement's longest continuous corporate partner, Coca-Cola has helped and shared in the evolution of the Olympic Games into the most watched and revered international event.'[1]
- Replica retro and vintage football shirts made by Toffs, 'The Old Fashioned Football Shirt Company', carry the wording '100% cotton, 100% nostalgia guaranteed' on their washing instructions.
- The Quorn Hunt's official website's 'About Us' section lists its current office holders alongside a list of its Former Masters going back to T. Boothby, who was appointed in 1698.[2]
- Martin Gough of the BBC quickly called the 2005 Ashes cricket series between England and Australia 'the greatest series ever'.[3] The prize-giving ceremony saw England captain Michael Vaughan receive an urn dating from 1882 containing the ashes of a cricket stump.
- Brentford FC's manager Martin Allen described his team's January 2005 FA Cup match against Hartlepool as 'the kind of blood and thunder game you got in the 1930s'.[4]

- In July 2005, Wade Boggs and Ryne Sandberg were inducted into the National Baseball Hall of Fame, joining the list of illustrious former players, managers, and umpires whose contributions to the game have been formally recognised. Boggs and Sandberg were the latest names on a list that goes back to the start of the Hall of Fame culture in 1936, when such greats as Ty Cobb, Babe Ruth, and Walter Johnson were honoured.[5]
- On 6 January 2006 – Old Christmas Day – the Fool in the Haxey Hood celebrations began this annual Lincolnshire event with the traditional cry of 'Hoose agen hoose, toon agen toon, if tha meets a man, nok im doon, but daon't ort im' ('House against house, town against town, if you meet a man, knock him down, but don't hurt him'). Teams from rival villages then attempted to propel the hood – a piece of rope wrapped in leather – to the designated goal, the door of the opposing village's pub. The exact origin of the game is unclear, but it is linked in local mythology to an incident in the thirteenth century, when villagers helped to retrieve the riding hood of a local woman after it was blown off in high winds.[6]

These diverse examples – and it would have been easy to have added many more – all illustrate an important feature of contemporary sport: the past features prominently in the present. This is not about academic interest in sports history: it is more about nostalgia, heritage, tradition, pride, and mythology, and about people's individual and communal sense of identity and belonging. In this chapter, we are going to explore some of the ways in which history – in its broadest sense – makes itself felt in sport. We will do this through three themes. First, we will look at the past as the place from which sport comes, the source of the ways in which we play. Second, we will look at the theme of sport and mythology, where the past is something we believe in as part of our engagement with sport. Finally, we will look at the past as something to commemorate and celebrate.

▶ 2.1 The past as the source of sport

The obvious starting point for our consideration of the presence of the past in contemporary sport is the basic, but easy to overlook, fact that all sports started at sometime in the past. No sports with which you are engaged started this morning: and even when there is a major development – say, the formulation of basketball in the 1890s, or emergence of wakeboarding in the 1980s – there is always something in the past to which we can make links. In all sports, it is relatively simple to move backwards from what we do now in order to find roots: from the various contemporary football codes to medieval football and Japanese *kemari*; from modern croquet to medieval *pelle melle*; from modern basketball to ancient *pok-tapok* from Yucatan; and from the unassisted speed-based sports of running and swimming to these same activities throughout human history. This is simply about recognising ancestry and family trees of sports as cultural activities. All sports have a history. They have all come from some points in the past, and the past influences many features of their current shape. Let us think through some of these.

2.1.1 Laws, rules, and organisations

Any attempt to define what it is that makes any given activity a sport will always include a reference to mutually agreed and bureaucratically enforceable rules. Without them we can have play, but not sport; and they are so central to our concept of sport that we simply take them for granted when we play, even if we try to break them for our advantage. As historians, we need to look beyond this, and look at their historical character. Every law and rule in every sport was created at a given moment, and was supported by enough people involved – players, coaches, officials, administrators, and so on – to tell us something about the sport's character at that time. Research will show the ways in which experimentation and evolution shaped rule-making within particular historical contexts, and those contexts will be evident for as long as the rules stand.

Let us consider a few examples. The laws of football as developed by the Football Association (FA) at its formation in 1863 were based on the version of the game as it had developed out of Cambridge University since the 1840s and Sheffield FC in the 1850s, and before that from various schools. The new rules brought together various traditions and cultures, and maintained the social character of amateurism through such concepts as 'fair play' and 'gentlemanly conduct'. In a related development, the breakaway Rugby Football Union (RFU), when it devised a separate set of rules from 1871, enshrined handling the ball and hacking as features of the sport that would distinguish it from what the FA were doing. Similarly, when the Northern Rugby Union (subsequently the Rugby Football League) broke away from the RFU in 1895, they quickly established new laws – relating both to players' finances and to features of the game, such as team sizes – that were more fitting to their increasingly working class catch-ments. Jack Broughton's London Prize Ring Rules of 1743 were devised to make pugilism safer after a fighter's death in the ring. They limited wrestling-style holds, for example, and barred punches below the belt. Later, changes under the Marquess of Queensberry in 1867 introduced further safety measures by regulating the length of rounds, insisting on good quality gloves, and setting a 10-second time limit on a fallen fighter being judged out rather than the more dangerous 30 seconds of Broughton's time.[7] These examples take us into such diverse issues as educational elitism, acceptable social behaviour, the management of finances, the tolerance of violence, and the safety of participants. A fuller analysis of rules would throw up many more themes. All of them are examples of specific historical contexts shaping the ways in which we play sport.

Activity 1: Recent influences on sports' laws

Various factors in various historical settings have influenced the evolution of sports' laws. The examples given above illustrate the role of such factors as financial protection and the control of violence. In recent decades, some of the most significant influences have been television, multiculturalism and the growth of an equal opportunities culture, and health and safety concerns and the related growth of litigation. Find evidence of these factors in the current rules and laws of as many sports as you can. You can find current laws on the official website of any sport's governing body. Tabulate your findings, and try to make connections and comparisons across the different sports.

As well as laws and rules, the organisations that regulate sport are all historical. They were all created at particular times by people with shared interests within the prevailing historical and cultural contexts, and these roots are evident in the way those organisations work in the present. In some cases, history and tradition are the most notable things about these organisations. In British sport, the key marker here is any organisation that uses the prefix 'royal' in its name, as this is evidence of both authority and tradition: the Royal and Ancient Golf Club, the Royal Caledonian Curling Club, the Royal Company of Archers, and the Royal Ocean Racing Club all have this historical statement embedded in their names, as do a number of clubs throughout the former British Empire, such as the Royal Calcutta Golf Club and the Royal Perth Yacht

Club. Other clubs, such as the Jockey Club in horse racing, the Maryle-bone Cricket Club in cricket, and the Hurlingham Club in polo, have also maintained both strong traditions and significant political power within their sports, thanks to their age. History is also evident in all sports' governing bodies, as the time of creation has entered into their cultures. This is particularly evident when we look at the wave of sports that developed associations or unions as their forms of governance in the period c.1860–1914. The Football Association (1863), the Rugby Football Union (1871), the Amateur Boxing Association (1880), the Amateur Swimming Association (1886): these are all period pieces. Despite various forms of modernisation, each one still has some semblance of the time of its birth, such as committee structures, forms of record keeping, notions of fair play and amateurism, and disciplinary cultures. The same can be said of all players' associations and trades union, ranging from the Professional Footballers Association (formed in 1907 as the Association Footballers' and Trainers' Union) to the Major League Baseball Players Association (1965). The reasons why the body was created – health insurance, earning potential, mutual aid, and so on – still characterise these organisations' working cultures. Yet again, history is inescapable.

2.1.2 Names

Another way in which we can see current sport as a product of the past is through names. The names of sports themselves are inherited from the past, and some of the apparent anomalies of naming can be understood only if we look to history. For either rugby code to call itself 'football' may seem incongruous to the newcomer due to the preponderance of handling over kicking in open play, but the name makes sense if you look at the sports' histories. Real tennis is no more or less 'real' than lawn tennis or table tennis: but a historical appreciation of language ('real' to mean 'royal', here, from the French), and a consideration of its players' desire to define their game as separate from the Victorian version's more bourgeois character, puts the name in context. Many sporting events have names that are shot through with history. The Derby in horse racing, run since 1780 and named after the patronage of the 12th Earl of Derby, and the label 'Olympic', used by Pierre de Coubertin for his multi-sporting event in the 1890s to stress his belief in the qualities of classical Greece, are two of the hundreds of historical names that remain in everyday use in contemporary sport. Historical names also abound at club level, seen clearest in British football culture, with many names still taking us into the community structures and urban landscapes of the Victorian period. The proliferation of Wanderers and Rovers, for example, reminds us of a boom in the numbers of football clubs without permanent homes, while the Uniteds maintain evidence of smaller clubs coming together. Sheffield Wednesday most perfectly keep alive into the twenty-first century the working week patterns of the late nineteenth century. One of the most famous English clubs, Arsenal, has a name that has no link to the part of North London in which they have been based since 1913, but instead maintains the tradition of their foundation in 1886 in the Woolwich Arsenal, an armaments factory in South London, with the cannon on their badge and their nickname of The Gunners reinforcing this historical link. In rugby union, the names of the various exiles' clubs – such as London Scottish (formed 1878), London Welsh (1885), and London Irish (1898) – keep alive not just national identity, but also the demographic circumstances and migration patterns of the periods in which they were created. Similar examples are evident across the world, from the German football club Schalke 04, who commemorate their year of foundation in the name, to the Richmond Alemannia Soccer Club in Australia, who stress their origins in the German community in their name. Finally in this context, we can look at sports' trophy cabinets for evidence of names inherited from the past being known by any sport's current enthusiasts. Sailing's most important trophy, the America's Cup, is named after *America*, the first yacht to win it in 1851. Australian state cricket teams have competed for the Sheffield Shield since 1893, named after patron Lord Sheffield; while a Victorian Governor-General of Canada, Lord Stanley, is remembered in North America's most prestigious ice hockey trophy. In ways such as this, names that made perfect sense in the past – names about time, geography, or patronage – but have since lost their contexts have stayed constant in sport, a key feature of sport's historical character.

Activity 2: Who were Lady Byng and Edgar Mobbs?

Many sporting events and competitions are named after people from the past. Some are named after sportsmen or women; but they are more often named after patrons. The list below names some of them, and the sports in which they are awarded. For each one, find out who the person was, when the event took the person's name, and why people within the sport at that time would have wanted to commemorate that person. Do the sport's current followers know anything about the person being commemorated? What are the differences between this sort of trophy naming and the commercial sponsorship of trophies, such as cricket's Benson and Hedges Cup?

Boxing   Lonsdale Belt
Canadian Football   Grey Cup
Cricket   Ranji Trophy
Croquet   MacPherson Shield
Field hockey   Beighton Cup
Golf   Ryder Cup
Ice hockey   Lady Byng Memorial Trophy; Calder Memorial Trophy
Indoor bowls   Aird Trophy
Lawn tennis   Davis Cup; Wightman Cup
Rugby Union   Edgar Mobbs Memorial Match; Currie Cup
Shooting   Pershing Trophy

2.1.3 Language

All sports contain their own technical language and insider's jargon.[8] This has two main purposes. First, it helps each sport's followers label increasingly specialised features, such as equipment or types of play: where an outsider sees a fielder on a cricket pitch, an insider sees a gully, a second slip, or a silly mid-on; where an outsider sees a sailing boat, an insider sees a 470, a Finn, or a catamaran. Second, the language helps to define the insider from the outsider, and helps to create a shared identity for insiders through vocabulary. In all sports, the language used contains historical elements: as with the names exemplified above, much specialised language has come out of each sport's past, and it cannot be fully understood unless that past is known. This can be seen in the languages which influence the official usage in sports. Think of fencing's reliance on French (*épée, piste, doighte*), of judo's use of Japanese (*judoka, kyu, dan, shiai, ippon*), or the prevalence of English in global football, where Japanese commentators call a penalty a 'p-kick', South American clubs call themselves Old Boys, Corinthians, Wanderers, and Juniors, and one of Italy's top teams uses the English spelling of its city's name, Milan, rather than the native Milano. It can also be seen in the specialised terms used in all sports, whether it be the bosey in cricket named after B.J.T. Bosanquet, who first used it in 1903; the axel in ice skating, named after Norwegian skater Axel Paulsen; or the garryowen in rugby union, named after Garryowen RFC, who first used the tactic. Sport, then, like any other cultural activity, displays its history through its language.

Activity 3: Language of origin

The following are words from various languages that are regularly used in specific sports. Find out each word's language of origin and meaning, and discuss the reasons why they are still in use within their sports. Bear in mind that some sports have taken words from more than one language.

Hurling   caman, sliothar
Kendo   hakama, shinai
Pelota   cancha, jaï-alaï
Real tennis   bisque tournée, paumier
Rowing   repêchage, regatta
Show jumping   barème, puissance
Skiing   vorlage, fraspark, schuss

2.1.4 Places

Another theme to set up here when considering the presence of the past in sport is to look at the locations at which sport is played. Where sports are played in the present tells us a great deal about their historical development. Ancient sports sites have usually been abandoned and, if they survive, do so as archaeology. However, in some settings there is a strong link with ancient sites, notably in the continued use of Roman amphitheatres in southern France for bullfighting. This usage can be seen at Arles, Nimes, and elsewhere, where each arena's antiquity is obvious. If we look at the sports that developed in the seventeenth and eighteenth centuries in the British Isles, we can see that some spaces dedicated to sport are still in use, notably in the racecourses of Newmarket and the golf course at St Andrew's. The past is firmly alive for anyone who competes or watches at these spaces, a past driven home in such localised names as the Rowley Mile at Newmarket, taken from Charles II's nickname, and the Old Course at St Andrew's. We are still living with the spaces built for the boom in urban sports from the late nineteenth century. In the UK, football grounds such as Aston Villa's Villa Park in Birmingham and Liverpool FC's Anfield are still in use, situated in the tight confines of Victorian residential areas. Many British greyhound and speedway stadiums are also still located in the urban communities they first served, as in Sheffield and Portsmouth. Recent stadium building has tended to be outside city centres, itself evidence of a new, post-industrial historical trend that has given us such locations as Houston's Astrodome and post-Taylor Report football stadiums in Sunderland, Bolton, and Reading. Altogether, the places in which we play and watch sport tell us something about the sport's development over time.

2.1.5 Access and etiquette

Even the most cursory look at contemporary sport shows that while opportunities for playing may be growing throughout the world, not all sports are available on an equal basis to all people. Some sports require participants to have significant disposable resources at their command. These resources include such tangible ones as time, money, and space, as well as less tangible cultural resources such as the knowledge of how to behave in certain situations and experience in certain forms of etiquette. This is best illustrated by contrasting the financial and the cultural resources needed to play polo with those needed to play darts or pool. While patterns of access can and do change over time, they are heavily influenced by historical patterns of access, and by perceptions of sports that are inherited from the past. These patterns are, in part, influenced by the traditions that sports choose to maintain and highlight. Dress codes in lawn tennis clubs and golf clubs, the use of the adjective 'royal' in certain sporting events (such as Henley Royal Regatta and Royal Ascot), and the use of particular terms of address (such as the All England Lawn Tennis and Croquet Club's continued usage of titles indicating women players' marital status in the Wimbledon Championships[9]) are all pieces of everyday history that help to perpetuate image and reality. Acts such as these help to stress tradition for those on the inside, while excluding those outside the sport who do not feel comfortable with that particular code of behaviour. There are also more tangible relationships between current access patterns in sports and their historical ones. Lawn tennis and croquet emerged in their modern forms in the second half of the nineteenth century, specifically as games that could be played on the lawns of people with grounds or large private gardens, and the clubs that supported these sports inevitably developed in socially exclusive areas, such as the new suburbs of London and Birmingham. Moreover, they were designed as sports that both sexes could play together, which meant for the Victorians that they could not be too physically strenuous for women. Without wishing to reduce everything to history, it is clear that there is a strong relationship between these sports' origins as mixed sex games for upper-middle-class leisure time, and their current structures and cultures. Using this model, we can look at any sport's historical development to see how closely it was linked to any particular groups within society, whether those groups were defined in terms of class, occupation, sex, age, ethnicity, or any other factor. In the British model, many sports had cultures that overlapped some of these boundaries: association football and horse racing are great examples, with their aristocracy of patrons and credit bettors, their bourgeoisie of managers, directors, owners, and disseminators, and their working class of labourers (such as players, jockeys, and stable workers), spectators, and cash bettors. The influence of these historical patterns remains strong in all sports' presents, and we cannot understand issues of access and inequality unless we look to history.

2.1.6 Records

Allen Guttmann's seminal study of sport, *From Ritual to Record*, analysed the ways in which sports have moved away from their religious origins and taken on secular roles. One of the characteristics of modern sports culture that he isolated as differentiating it from ancient parallels was the status of the record:

> When we can no longer distinguish the sacred from the profane or even the good from the bad, we content ourselves with minute discriminations between the batting average of the .308 hitter and the .307 hitter. Once the gods have vanished from Mount Olympus or Dante's paradise, we can no longer run to appease them or to save our souls, but we can set a new record. It is a uniquely modern form of immortality.[10]

The cult of sports records that this quotation identifies is another way in which the past informs the present in sport. Some sports are more record-obsessed than others, but all sports have a cult of their own specific record holders – the fastest, strongest, highest, most successful, and so on, depending on the sport. The names of the first to complete certain activities are celebrated even outside each sport, with, for example, the triumphs of Roger Bannister (the first runner to cover a mile in under four minutes, in 1954) and Matthew Webb (the first person to swim across the English Channel, in 1875) still known widely outside of athletics and swimming respectively. Records such as this are celebrated for what they tell us about human potential and athletic discipline, and are maintained as a way of seeing how far we have come: here, history is something that we are aware of because we are, to use Nancy Struna's simple but effective phrase, 'moving away from' it.[11] Enthusiasts who maintain accounts of the high achievers in their sports, and who update these records when they fall, demonstrate the vitality of the past as a shaping influence on the sporting present.

There are countless other ways in which the past informs the present in sport. The past is present for every runner who maintains records of personal bests, for every gambler who considers a horse's pedigree and form before placing a bet, for every league in any sport that is based on past performance, for every cup winner who kisses the trophy in the way that previous winners have done, for every fan who carries out a familiar ritual on the day of a match hoping that it will bring good luck, and for every collector of baseball cards or football programmes. The past is the source of sport.

▶ 2.2 Sport and mythology

Another reason why we should study the history of sport links to an important feature of most sports' own engagement with the past. It should be clear by now that many sports' establishments care about the past of their own sport: they simply would not name trophies after heroes, maintain traditions, or preserve old laws if the past was irrelevant to them. This does not mean that they cannot be forward-looking and interested in change and innovation, too: it is just that the past matters as a part of their identity. However, it is also clear that many sports are relatively narrow-minded when it comes to history: they tend to see what they want to see, and to ignore or marginalize less comfortable aspects, or features which contradict their preferred view. This is particularly evident when major changes have occurred, and sports administrators rewrite what went before to make it fit with the new situation. The early years of the modern Olympic movement provide an excellent example, analysed so thoroughly by David Young in *The Modern Olympics*. Young shows that there were a number of multi-sport events that used the name 'Olympic' or 'Olympian' throughout the nineteenth century, based variously in Greece, England, and France; and Pierre de Coubertin was working within a long tradition. However, he quickly became seen as the founder of the Olympics, and his prede-cessors were written out of Olympic history.[12] This is history as written by the victors to explain and justify their victory, and it is written without the self-reflection that most historians now recognise as fundamental to their study. However, we cannot simply dismiss sports' readings of their own past because they are misleading: we need to go further. It is crucial to see what parts of the past sports promote, as this helps us to understand their identities and how they see themselves in the present.

What we can do, then, is to consider sport's own engagement with its past as being mythologised. This does not mean that it is based on things that did not happen: we are using the concept of mythology in a more sophisticated sense than that. Looking at myths in this setting is about looking at the selective bits of the past that people want to remember, and at the ways in which people construct particular stories out of them. This is something that we can see in many aspects of human life beyond sport. All major religions have creation myths, for example, which take elements from a real past and develop a religious narrative around them. Societies also develop political, military, and social myths, based around attractive and usually simplistic readings of particular events from the past. Sport is no different: and through looking at some sports' own myths, and at the way they present the past as leading inevitably to their own preferred present, we can get a sense of what history means to those sports' enthusiasts and establishments.

2.2.1 Creation myths

Any basic engagement with history will show that all sports have evolved over time. Even those that can claim specific moments of inven-tion in particular forms, such as basketball's creation by James Naismith in 1891, have precedents in earlier forms of play. In the case of basket-ball, for example, John Arlott has shown similarities not just with sacred games played in South America in the seventh century BC, but has also noted the eleventh-century Persian poet Omar Khayyam's words: 'You are a ball, played with by fate; a ball which God throws since the dawn of time into the catch-basket.'[13] Ultimately, all sport can be seen to have roots in certain activities, notably running, swimming, throwing, catching, kicking, and hunting, as well as in displays of physical strength against other people, animals, or on inanimate objects. Most sports acknowledge the varied roots of their particular game. As Percy Young put it in his popular history of football, 'a historian knows that to speak of any phenomenon as being the first of its kind is either impossible, or impolitic, or both'.[14] However, despite this sensible view, there has been a significant trend, especially in the nineteenth century, for sports to claim specific moments of birth. These are sports' creation myths.

The two most famous examples are probably the 1823 William Webb Ellis story in rugby and the 1839 Abner Doubleday story in baseball. Eric Dunning, Joseph Maguire, and Robert Pearton have argued that belief in these myths is 'a kind of sports equivalent of the belief in the tooth fairy or Father Christmas'.[15] In the case of rugby, Jonathan Rice has provided us with an excellent digest of the myth's development.[16] Contemporary records from the 1820s showed that handling and running with the ball were developing as features of the version of football played at Rugby School, but no one recorded who had first had the idea of playing this way. When the laws were published in 1846, handling was clearly part of the game. When the clubs that preferred the running and handling style split from the kickers at the Football Association in 1871, they did not promote any particular story about how the distinctive style had started; and two books on the history of the game published in 1885 and 1892 respectively did not mention Webb Ellis. The story of a key moment in 1823 when Webb Ellis is supposed to have ignored the rules by picking up the ball and running with it was not produced until the 1890s, 70 years after it is supposed to have happened. The timing is the point of the story: this was the decade in which association football became dominated by professionalism in the leading clubs, and when a number of rugby clubs in the north of England were pressing for some financial incentives for players, either broken time payments or open professionalism. Under this type of pressure, a middle-class sport which wished to stress its clean, amateur roots found it convenient to do so by inventing a story about a moment of inspired individualism in one of the country's leading schools. The myth became immensely popular within the rugby establishment, formalised in stone in 1923, when a plaque commemorating Webb Ellis' 'fine disregard for the rules', one hundred years earlier, was erected in Rugby School, later joined by a statue. The continued popularity of the story can be seen in the fact that some rugby enthusiasts evidently still believe it, and it has survived as a straightforward historical fact in some popular history. For example, Clem Thomas, a former international who wrote a history of the British Lions in 1996, discussed the 1888 idea of a British representative team as having happened '65 years after William Webb Ellis had invented the game which took the name of his school'.[17] The myth also survives at the sport's highest level, where the World Cup is named the Webb Ellis Trophy.

In the USA, baseball has a similar creation myth, with Abner Doubleday of Cooperstown, New York, credited with inventing the sport in 1839. As with the rugby union example, this version of the sport's origins was established by committee in the early years of the twentieth century, when the Mills Commission (1905–07) settled on Doubleday as the founder. This came at a time when the baseball establishment wished to distance itself from the allegation that their sport was simply an adaptation of the English children's game of rounders. His adaptations to generic bat and ball games – notably the use a diamond-shaped area with bases at each angle – were seen as proof that the game was all-American and manly, not English and juvenile. This version became the accepted story, and the sport's centenary was accordingly celebrated in 1939. As with Webb Ellis, the myth has come under attack from historians, and its shortcomings are now recognised by the National Baseball Hall of Fame. Nevertheless, it continues to influence the game's historical image, not least in the baseball heritage tourism centred on Cooperstown, and in the continued dating of baseball's anniversaries from 1839.[18] Creation myths such as these serve the purpose of telling a sport's followers where the sport has come from. They can variously offer age, heritage, social legitimacy, and national identity. Whatever their function, such myths show one of the ways in which sports present their own history.

Activity 4: Myths and their modern believers

The William Webb Ellis and the Abner Doubleday stories continue to have their believers, despite their dubious accuracy. Using popular histories, reference books, and club and governing body websites for one of these sports, find five references to either Webb Ellis or Doubleday. How are the stories presented in these sources? How far do the authors appear to believe in the myths? Why are these stories still popular?

2.2.2 Continuity and the 'invention of tradition'

Mythologising the past is also evident in narratives of continuity and evolution that are rife in sport. Any number of authors of popular histories of sport, particularly those who publish on the Internet, draw direct lines between ancient play and their favourite sport. However, this trend is not limited to the opportunities for bad history writing that the World Wide Web offers. As with creation myths, it is something in which a number of sports' establishments have engaged. It is sport's version of a trend that Eric Hobsbawm and Terence Ranger described as 'the invention of tradition'.[19] As the contributors to Hobsbawm and Ranger's collection *The Invention of Tradition* showed, institutions as diverse as the monarchy and Scottish nationalists all have produced dubious historical traditions for themselves in order to stress their age and legitimacy. Various sports' establishments and enthusiasts have similarly invented continuities and traditions. Some of the stories strike us as comical from the start, such as the legend promoted by some of the nineteenth-century enthusiasts of the Gaelic sport of shinty (*camanach*). Writing in the 1880s, a time when many sports were striving to establish their amateur roots and their antiquity, the True Highlanders took shinty back to Genesis:

> [I]t is said, and, no doubt, with great truth, that the game of *Camanachd*, or club playing, was introduced into the Green Isle [Great Britain] by the immediate descendants of Noah. On such authority we may rationally conclude that it was played by Noah himself; and if by Noah, in all probability by Adam and his sons.[20]

A similarly long-term approach, albeit to classical antiquity rather than to the Bible, is also present in some Olympic historiography. Many from within the International Olympic Committee (IOC) have, since its foundation in 1894, worked hard to present the Olympics not as the modern phenomenon that it is, reliant on such luxuries of the industrial age as international transport links, leisure time, organised physical education, and cross-border social and professional networks, but as a revival of the ancient games. There were – and are – some ancient trappings, such as the IOC's chosen nomenclature and the quadrennial calendar: but these were born out of the leaders' love of ancient Greece, not through any survival of a particular way of doing things over the millennium and a half between the ancient games' dissolution and the establishment of the modern Olympics. The modern trappings of Olympism – the sports involved, the strong role of nation states, the secular setting, the cosmopolitanism of the participants – far outweighed any ancient features, even in the 1890s. However, in a quest to establish legitimacy and authority, the ancient games form a frequent feature in modern Olympic history. Most recently, the 2004 Athens Olympics were presented as a return not just to the host city of the first Olympics of 1896, but as a return to the spiritual home of Olympism. Throughout modern Olympic history, this theme has been significant, as exemplified in Webster's

1914 book of Olympic history, staggeringly entitled *The Evolution of the Olympic Games, 1829 BC–1914 AD*.[21]

This type of approach gives each sport's followers a sense of tradition. This tells us far more about the beliefs of the people writing the history than it does about the past itself. In the case of the Olympics, this promotion of a mythologised tradition takes us into a range of ideologies and beliefs of some people in early twentieth-century Europe and North America, such as a fear of modernism and a belief in the spiritual and cultural supremacy of ancient civilizations. A good example is the torch relay from Olympia to the host city, now an established ritual in the Olympics: but far from the supposed antiquity of such a ritual, embodied in the allegedly classical clothing of the women who light the torch, the relay was created by the Nazi organisers of the 1936 Berlin Olympics. This invented tradition thus owes more to the Nazis' interest in ancient civilisations and their antipathy towards modernism than it does to any genuine Olympic tradition. The fact that all Olympic hosts since 1936 have taken it on as an ancient symbol rather than recognising it as a Nazi one forms an interesting sidelight on the invention of such traditions.

2.2.3 Golden ages

The same forces as those which lead sports to invent moments of creation and long-term traditions can be seen at work in any sport's promotion of its golden age. All major sports are deemed to have such periods, times when the game was at some kind of peak of development and performance without any corrupting features being present. As with other mythologies from within sport, golden ages bear deconstruction. First off, they are relative to the people looking back. Look at the absence of women from cricket's apparent golden age, of black athletes from athletics' golden age, of wheelchair participants from the golden age of the Olympics. All of these groups would come up with alternative golden ages that are meaningful to them. Golden ages can be similarly one-eyed when it comes to national groups. Referring to the England football team's two defeats by Hungary in 1953 and 1954 as the end of a golden age ignores the fact that it was the start of a golden age – albeit a short-lived one – for Hungarian football. Whenever faced with a golden age, it is the historian's job to ask who is doing the reminiscing, and for whom the age was golden. A second characteristic of golden ages is that they were rarely as free from the symbols of decline and corruption as their believers would wish. Olympic athletes used drugs at least as early as 1904, rugby union players received illegal payments throughout the game's amateur period from the 1870s to the 1990s, governments intervened in sports for political capital and diplomatic advantage from the start of modern sport, there was event sponsorship at the 1908 Olympic Games, cricket was dominated by gambling in its early days, and competitors in the ancient Olympics were effectively professionals. Historical research can quickly chip away the haloes that enthusiasts for golden ages would place on their heroes, and show them as human beings making choices about how they conducted themselves when they played. Research into contexts rather than merely contests can help us make sense of the presence of money, the media, politics, and cheating in any period of any sport's history. This is the basic work of the historian: to try to make sense of what happened in the past, based on its own evidence and our reading of it. The point here is to stress that a belief in golden ages, however naïve it may seem, is an important part of sport's own engagement with its past.

These sporting mythologies, based on creation, continuity, and golden ages, can be described as history, albeit history that is at best unconsciously subjective and at worst wholly fictional. However, this does not mean that academic historians should ignore these mythologies. Historians have to try to work out what happened. How did rugby union emerge as a distinct form of football throughout the nineteenth century, for example, or how did the founders of the Olympic Games disseminate their ideas? The myths outlined above tell us very little about what happened in this sense. However, historians also have a duty to look at what people believe about their situations, including how they interpret their own past. This is what John Tosh calls the 'quest for meaning' in history writing, a quest designed to help us see 'how people interpreted their world and represented their experience' as a 'matter of intrinsic interest'.[22] In this setting, the rugby union story about Webb Ellis and the Olympians' belief that their organisation owes more to ancient Greece than to nineteenth-century France are significant. They may not tell us what actually happened, but they tell us a great deal about the beliefs, attitudes, ideologies, and cultures of those whose actions and decisions we are studying. So, for example, the Webb Ellis story may tell us nothing about the 1820s, where it is set; but it tells us a great deal about the 1890s, when it was popularised. In this sense, we have to study sports' own myths as a way into their own views of the past. This can be challenging, especially if you have grown up believing in these myths. As Bernard Whimpress put it in his discussion of facts in sports history, 'myths often have a sense of wonder about them which hard facts will deny and the historian can appear as something of a spoil sport'.[23] However, the importance of tackling myths while finding out why people believe in them is central to academic sports history, and you should not shirk this responsibility.

▶ 2.3 Sport and heritage

A third theme to look at in this overall consideration of sport's historical nature is heritage and commemoration. Sport's past remains alive in diverse acts of remembrance and celebration that are woven into the lives and rituals of those involved with sport in the present. In these ways, sport can be seen as part of the heritage of many different types of community, including the family, the town or suburb, the city, the region, and the national and global communities of sports enthusiasts. Heritage, defined here as the preservation of something from the past in a way that is meaningful for the present and could be of interest in the future, figures heavily in sport. We can see this through sports museums, through the preservation of sites or the commemoration of sport when places are redeveloped, and in the recognition of individuals through road-naming, stadium-naming, and memorial statuary.

2.3.1 Museums

Sport is increasingly being represented in museums. This is most obvious when we see the growth of specialised museums devoted to particular sports or sporting organisations.[24] These are prevalent in the USA, where the long-standing hall of fame culture has given us such museums as those dedicated to baseball in Cooperstown, New York; basketball in Springfield, Massachusetts; and soccer in Oneonta, New York. English examples include the National Football Museum in Preston and the River and Rowing Museum and the Henley Museum in Henley-on-Thames, along with specialised collections linked to clubs and stadiums, as in the museums devoted to rugby union at Twickenham, lawn tennis at Wimbledon, and horse racing at Newmarket. In addition, many other museums with a wider remit are also increasingly including sports-based displays. This is evident in local history museums, where sport is covered in particular displays, and in specialised museums where sport can be seen as a minor part of the story: sport in the army at the National Army Museum and transport workers' sports clubs in the Glasgow Transport Museum are both examples of this. When we also include art exhibitions in this, such as the National Portrait Gallery's Sporting Heroes exhibition of 1998–99, we can see a significant interest in sport from the museum and gallery sector. Such spaces are, as Wray Vamplew has put it, 'sports history's public face'.[25] However, as Robert Hewison argues in his *The Heritage Industry*, museums are not neutral places: 'A display in a museum may simply be telling a story, but the existence of a museum has a story to tell.'[26] The story to be told from the growth of the museum industry's interest in sport is that sport's past matters. The growth in museumisation is underpinned by the assumption that sport's past – both the physical artefacts that fit into display cases and the memories and stories that such artefacts can inspire – should not be allowed to die out. This trend is, of course, open to criticism. Who chooses which parts of sport's past should be museumised? Does the growth of museums suggest a feeling of insecurity about the future? How can commercial, community, and academic interests all be served by any particular sports museum? Would resources spent on museums be better devoted to developing sport for the future? Wherever we stand on these issues, we need to recognise that sport is now taken seriously by museums, another sign of the presence of the past in contemporary sports culture.

Activity 5: From running track to display case

Sports museums, like museums dedicated to any other theme, collect artefacts that can be linked to famous individuals from the past. The link between object and hero gives the artefact an elevated status, turning it into a secular relic. For example, British Olympic double gold medallist Kelly Holmes, who was in the army before making a full-time career in athletics, has one of her running vests displayed in the National Army Museum. Objectively, there is no difference between this vest and any other army running vest from that period: but the fact that Holmes wore it makes it special. Using a reliable internet search engine, locate the museums in which the following artefacts are held.

- The Washington Senators' baseball cap worn by pitcher Walter Johnson during the 1926 season.

- The shoes worn by Carl Lewis in the final of the 200 metres at the 1984 Los Angeles Olympic Games.

- Ski Jumper Matti Nykänen's medal collection.

- The shirt worn by England's Arnold Kirke-Smith in the first football inter-national, the England v Scotland match of 1872.

- The ice hockey net in which Wayne Gretzky of the LA Kings scored his National Hockey League record-breaking 802nd goal.

- Fishhooks dropped on the pitch of Lancaster Park, Christchurch, by anti-apartheid protesters during the 1981 South African rugby union tour of New Zealand.

What does this significance by association tell us about sporting celebrity? Why do sports enthusiasts revere some items but not others? What should the relationship between museums, private collectors, auction houses, and the famous sportsperson's family be?

2.3.2 Sites

Towards the end of the twentieth century, stadium development in many countries set up interesting questions about the heritage of sports sites. Many sports places were no longer suitable for the demands of the sports that they had been built for: health and safety concerns (espe-cially, in the UK, after the 1989 Hillsborough disaster), the changing demographics of crowds, the technical demands of media companies, and new accessibility requirements all meant that many clubs had to choose between closing sections of their grounds, redeveloping them, or selling up and relocating. Different clubs took different solu-tions. In the debates about those solutions, sporting heritage began to be discussed seriously. In England, the heritage organisation English Heritage became involved, and helped to promote the idea that sports sites – not just professional football clubs' grounds, but also everything from pub bowling greens to Victorian swimming baths – should be open to the same kind of interest as the more traditional sites of heritage investment and tourism, such as castles, ruined abbeys, and stately homes. The interests of heritage have to be balanced against those of the present, and the constantly developing needs of health and safety requirements in sports sites create a tension between those who would seek to preserve and those who would update to keep a site functional. Some of the results may be compromises, but there have been some imaginative attempts to maintain a sense of sport's past, once a site has become obsolete.[27] This has been demonstrated in the ways in which professional football clubs' nineteenth sports grounds have been redeveloped once they have moved to new, twenty-first-century homes. In many, where housing or retail interests have taken over the old site, various architectural and design steps have been taken to remember sport. At The Dell, Southampton FC's home from 1898 until 2001, the property developers used a

> specific design approach . . . to preserve some of the great memories by echoing the layout of the Dell. The four sided arrangement of the homes evokes the spectators [sic] stands. These surround a central landscaped courtyard which itself is on the exact site of the old pitch and indeed the old centre spot.[28]

Roads and buildings within the complex have been named after players and managers, such as Le Tissier Court and Ted Bates Court. In this way, sports sites that are no longer economically viable can be converted for a new economic activity without the sport associated with the site being forgotten. This is an exciting new development in sports history, and one that shows a strong link between past and present in the sporting public's perception. English Heritage's interest in sport, evident in its involvement in the Played in Britain project, is an example of this growing interest in sport's material heritage being taken seriously.[29]

2.3.3 Public commemoration

Public commemoration does not just focus on naming roads after club heroes in converted football grounds. Beyond this, sport's past is kept through diverse forms of public remembrance. Some clubs name parts of their grounds, or the ground itself, after famous players, coaches, or administrators from the past, such as the Tom Finney Stand at Preston North End FC's Deepdale, or Real Madrid's Santiago Bernebau Stadium. As well as naming, many sports figures have had statues erected to them at meaningful sites, such as Reg Harris at the Velodrome in Manchester, Fred Perry inside the All-England Club at Wimbledon, Bill Shankly at Liverpool FC's Anfield, and Paavo Nurmi outside Helsinki's Olympic Stadium. Nor is this limited to people: Red Rum, the horse that won the Grand National three times in the 1970s, has a statue at Aintree, and is buried near the winning post. However, this trend has not been confined to the stadium or its precincts itself, and sportsmen – and, to a lesser degree, women – have been commemorated within their communities, or communities in which they made an impact, in various ways. The two major media for such remembrance have been statues and street names, with sports figures encroaching on areas that were previously the preserve of royal, military, artistic, political, and religious figures. Again, any list can only scratch the surface of this trend. Statues to athlete Fanny Blankers-Koen in Amsterdam, boxer Joe Louis in Detroit, and footballer Stanley Matthews in Stoke-on Trent are all examples of this. At least one sporting animal has gone one better than statuary: 1930s greyhound racing legend Mick the Miller not only has an enclosure named after him at Wimbledon Stadium, but has his stuffed remains on display in the Rothschild Natural History Museum at Tring. Beyond statuary, the naming of roads after significant sportsmen and women often affords public recognition. As with statues, this tends to happen in the communities where the people made their biggest impact. Rugby league legend Clive Sullivan has the Clive Sullivan Way in Kingston Upon Hull, while Alf Ramsey is remembered by Sir Alf Ramsey Way in Ipswich, where he was Ipswich Town FC's leading manager. Similarly, Jesse Owens Strasse, dedicated in 1984 after the 1936 Olympic hero's death, is close to the scene of his triumphs in Berlin. This trend is ubiquitous, with the commemoration of sporting heroes now a part of the fabric of the urban community. In addition, memorials are often erected to people who have died in or around sporting events. From teams, such as the members of the Manchester United team killed in an air crash in 1958, through to spectators killed in crowd disasters as at Hillsborough in 1989, and Heysel and Valley Parade in 1985, and individuals who died as a direct result of sporting activity, such as cyclist Tommy Simpson in 1967: all of these dead have some kind of memorial erected to them, either at the site of the death or in the fabric of relevant stadiums. As with military memorials, these serve to remind us in the present of sacrifices – usually accidental, always tragic – made by people in the past of our sports. The fact that many of these memorials continue to serve as a focus for people's grief years after the events suggests a dynamic relationship between past and present.

Activity 6: The aviator, the casino owner, and the politician

Despite the growing trend of commercial sponsorship of stadiums, many stadiums are also named after people as an act of commemoration. Those honoured are often players, officials, and coaches, but figures from other occupations — such as business, politics, religion, or the armed forces — also have sports places named for them. Below are a few examples, some sporting, some not. In each case, find out who the person being honoured was, and discuss the reasons why a stadium was named after him.

- Bobby Dodd Stadium, Atlanta, USA

- Casement Park, Belfast, Northern Ireland

- Croke Park, Dublin, Ireland

- Fritz Walter Stadium, Kaiserslauten, Germany

- Mário Filho Stadium, Rio de Janeiro, Brazil

- Paul Brown Stadium, Cincinnati, USA

- Rod Laver Arena, Melbourne, Australia

- Roland Garros Stadium, Paris, France

- Sam Boyd Stadium, Las Vegas, USA

- Spyros Louis Stadium, Athens, Greece

- The Stoop Memorial Ground, Twickenham, England

- Tofig Bakhramov Stadium, Baku, Azerbaijan.

▶ 2.4 Conclusion

The themes covered in this chapter, and the examples chosen to illustrate them, demonstrate one of the assumptions underlying this book: that sport in the present cares about its past. History is all around us when we engage with sport. This fact informs the sports historian's critical agenda. If any sport's past is left as something taken for granted, then it can never be understood. Therefore, sports history is about looking beyond the myths and marketing, the statues and traditions, and finding out – as far as we can – what sport was like in the past, and the ways in which the past informs the present Sports history gocs bcyond the simple narratives and looks at sport in the round. Having devoted this chapter to the relationship between history and sport, and the ways in which the past informs the present, we shall move on to look in the next chapter at ways in which history as an academic discipline has engaged with sport.

3 Sport and Historiography

In Chapter 1, we looked briefly at some of the debates that go on around the nature of history. Out of that discussion, we can see a distinction between history as the past and history as the stuff that historians write. Studying the second type – that is, looking at historians' work rather than just reading it to find out what happened – is called historiography, the theme of this chapter. To take historiography seriously requires you to acknowledge the role of relativism in history writing. Studying historians' writings is a way of finding out about ideology's role in the discipline, and a way of seeing how the history that gets written is always linked to the time and the place in which it was created. If we accept this, then historiography becomes a vital project. Historiography is concerned with how historians work, and why they do particular types of work at particular times. It is concerned with debates in history writing, and with the ways in which social, political, and cultural trends – such as Marxism, feminism, or multiculturalism – influence the ways in which historians work. Doing historiography is essential if we hope to understand the past, as it helps us to see behind the assumptions, judgements, and results of previous historical research.

▶ 3.1 The role of historiography

Many areas of history now have their own devoted historiographers, scholars who explore the shifting trends in the writing about the subject over generations and between different countries. The work that these scholars produce helps other historians, including students, to see the ways in which contextual factors affect the writing of history. Beyond sports history, for example, Roger Richardson has done this with historical accounts of the English Civil War, while Michael Marrus has explored the shifting debate around the Holocaust through historians' writings.[1] An accessible sporting example can be found in Daniel Nathan's *Saying It's So*, an analysis of how baseball's 1919 World Series scandal has been reinterpreted, represented, and remembered by historians and others (such as novelists and film-makers) over the years. Nathan looks at ways in which contemporary concerns of the time of production have influenced the telling of the story.[2] This is historiography. It is the act of putting a piece of writing about history into the context of the time and the place in which it was written, and of recognising the role of the author's biography, career, and ideology.

The relevance of this for our current project is that if we do not think historiographically about the sports history we read, we will be detaching that literature from its context. The texts you read – books, articles, Internet sites, and so on – will make far more sense when you read them in the light of their discipline, and when you develop the skills to identify key authors, debates, ideologies, trends, and influences, than if you simply read them at face value. Through this approach, we can see how the climate of the historian's time has had an impact on the sports history he or she writes, and we can judge work by its own standards rather than by some later criteria. This is different from the approach you may be used to with scientific literature, where the pace of research means that you are always on the look out for the most recent material. For example, if you were working on sports nutrition then you would not find much value in a book from 1900, before the isolation of vitamins and the understanding of their importance. Findings do change over time in history writing, particularly when new evidence is found, and when new theories are applied to old issues; but there is also a strong tendency to respect and value older material, and not to marginalise it. It is only through thinking historiographically that we can achieve this.

Another point to make before looking at the growth of a distinct history of sport is that the subject matter of history is always evolving. History as a discipline may be about the past, but it is rooted in the present: and the things about which people want to know change with contemporary tastes, fashions, and needs. For example, the history of organised religion is always vital to any religious society, but declines in significance in secular times. Indeed, the way in which religious history in the UK has gone from being about the history of organised Christianity to being more encompassing of other faiths and traditions is indicative of how the needs of the present help to define the subject matter of history. Politics has long been a staple area of historical research, as has war, and political and military history remain popular as they help people to understand the roots of so many parts of their national traditions and obligations. Social and economic history have grown in importance in mass societies.[3] Some historians have drawn attention to the links between their historical writing and the times in which they were living. Richard Evans, for example, made an explicit statement of this in his work on the history of disease. In *Death in Hamburg* of 1987, he drew parallels between the cholera epidemics of the nineteenth century that formed the subject matter of the book and contemporary issues of the time of writing:

> Nearly ten thousand people died in this disaster ... and the ways in which the city coped, or failed to cope, with the catastrophe, and the effects it had on the life of the city afterwards, have parallels and lessons for the medical problems and urban disasters of a century later, in the ages of AIDS and the nuclear peril.[4]

This is not just a useful way to think about the links between the history that gets written and the time and the place in which it is written. It can also help us to understand the timing and popularity of any branch of history, such as sports history.

We need to appreciate this aspect of historical writing if we are to understand the reasons for the growth of sports history. This can give us an appreciation of some aspects of the historiography that might have seemed random before. Why was women's sport virtually ignored by the first generation of British sports historians? Look at the gender profile of the historians, and the relatively small influence that feminism had on history writing at the time. Why have American sports historians given Jewish sports history far more attention than their British counterparts? Look at the relative sizes of the Jewish populations in both countries, and the higher profile of specifically Jewish sporting culture in the USA than the UK. Why has the theme of sport and national identity been more important in the sports history written in Australia and Scotland than it has in England? Unless we think historiographically, and put texts in context, we will always leave an obstacle between us and the texts that we read. The history we get we deserve: and the history that gets written, in sport as in any other area, is heavily influenced by our concerns in the present.

We are back to Southgate's claim, quoted in Chapter 1, that unexamined history is not worth studying. Part of the examination of history that you need to be prepared to do is historiographical. This chapter is designed to give you a foundation in this skill. It will do so by looking at the relationship between history as an academic discipline and sport as a subject matter, exploring the timing of sports history's birth and growth as a sub-discipline, and looking at why the academic world developed its interest in sport at this time. The issues covered here will enhance your skills of reading history texts critically, and they will help you to approach every text you use in an academic frame of mind.

▶ 3.2 The growth of sports history

The main focus of this book is academic sports history. What do we mean by the academic world? What agencies and organisations make up what, in shorthand, we call the history establishment? We need to think about the nature of this establishment, so that we can understand something about the timing of its relationship with sport. Broadly, and in any subject area, the academic establishment is made up of university departments, subject-specific associations complete with their own national and international networks of conferences and journals, the academic publishing industry, and professional bodies. The nature and identity of the different agencies vary from subject to subject and from country to country, but there is always an interrelationship between these groups. Through various channels – degrees and other educational courses, books, journals, media work, professional standards – each subject area's establishment effectively dominates discourse on that particular subject. For history, the key agencies are perhaps less obvious than those in such areas as law and medicine, where the public face of the subject is highly visible on a daily basis. However, history still has its own establishment, and the interplay between the different agencies helps to define the terms and limits of the subject. The key agencies are university history departments and examination boards, historical societies and associations (such as Institute of Historical Research, the Royal Historical Society, the American Historical Association, and the Royal Australian Historical Society), academic and general publishers with an interest in history, the archive industry, and the relevant parts of the museum, heritage, and library services. This is not an attempt to make out that there is some kind of secret society dictating historical taste. However, we need to see how the cultural and professional positioning of these agencies help to define what gets taken seriously – which areas of history are studied, what kind of historians have their research funded, what kind of books get published, what kind of books and journals get collected by university libraries, what kind of sources get collected by professional archives – and what gets ignored. To understand the growth of sports history, we have to see how sport as a subject matter has gradually shifted from being ignored to being taken seriously.

Activity 1: Noting the spread of sports history

The history of sport is now taken seriously in many parts of what we can loosely call the history establishment. Using a reliable search engine, find evidence of how this is currently taking place by finding an example of sports history in one of each of the following types of institutions:

- A pre-university educational programme from the country in which you are studying

- A pre-university educational programme from another country

- A university from the country in which you are studying

- A university from another country

- An academic publishing company

- A national heritage organisation

- A non-sporting museum

- An academic research grant awarding body.

There are a number of good accounts of how sports history has emerged as a sub-discipline of history, and as a part of the multidisciplinary subject area of sports studies. Richard Holt, William Baker, Peter Bailey, Jeffrey Hill, Martin Polley, Martin Johnes, and others have outlined the main stages in British sports history.[5] Other traditions covered include Daryl Adair, Richard Cashman, and Bernard Whimpress on Australasia,[6] Nancy Struna, Steven Riess, and Steven Pope on the USA,[7] Arnd Krüger on Germany,[8] and Joseph Arbena on Latin America.[9] You should supplement this literature, which outlines and analyses the development of sports historiography, with Richard Cox's comprehensive and invaluable bibliographies, which list thousands of publications.[10] From surveys such as these, we can broadly identify a number of reasons why sport became a legitimate and increasingly popular area for historians during the second half of the twentieth century.

3.2.1 Non-academic antecedents

History – including sports history – is not written only by professional academics. A vast body of literature exists that has been written by non-academic historians, people who do not make their living working in history departments, and who often come to the materials without the professional training of postgraduate research. It can be hard to distinguish this type of material, and you will need to read around in both genres to develop a feel for how they differ. Broadly, non-academic books tend to be heavy on detail and low on context, and often lack the transparent referencing of sources that academic work demands. Although the focus of this book is on helping you develop the skills needed to be an academic sports historian, it would be naive and elitist to ignore the vast body of historical literature written over the years by diverse non-academic authors who were interested in the past of their favourite sports. This material may not be classed as academic, either now or by the standards of the time in which it was written; and the authors, rather than being lecturers or academically funded researchers, were enthusiasts, journalists, administrators, and participants. Such work may lack the academic's concerns with contexts: but without it, much of the narrative of how certain sports evolved, what they were like at given moments, and who the key people and organisations were would now be lost. The quality of this type of literature varies: we will be looking at some examples in Chapter 4, and we should remember here the frankly nonsensical claims that some such books contain, as exemplified in Chapter 2 with the claim that Adam and Eve played shinty in the Garden of Eden. Such mythologies apart, for the decades in which academic historians did not think sport a worthy subject matter, other people were writing sports history according to their lights.

This diverse body of literature is particularly strong on local and regional histories of various sports, and on the histories of clubs and organisations. The coverage is diverse, patchy, and highly selective. Not every sport found its pre-academic historian, while some sports had many. Typically, hunting, shooting, and fishing were well served by such historians, at both national and local levels. Many hunts have had their own chroniclers and historians, while enthusiasts of other field sports would write up the history of their favourite areas. As we saw with our discussion of the invention of tradition in Chapter 2, one of the motives behind such historiography was each author's desire to stress legitimacy, heritage, and tradition for his or her favourite activity. Pierce Egan's *Boxiana* of 1812, Pelham Warner's *The Book of Cricket* of 1911, and Theodore Cook's three-volume *A History of the English Turf* of 1905 are a few examples of this genre of sports history written by partisan historians long before they drew the attention of academics.[11] The Badminton Library of Sports and Pastimes of 1885 was crucial here, as were the local studies of sport contained in the Victoria County History of England series from 1899. These histories give us details of characters, heroes, landscapes, social networks, and sporting events. This non-academic tradition continues, and should not be ignored by academic historians.

3.2.2 The widening territory of history

Academic history broadly ignored sport until the 1960s. It was left to each sport's in-house enthusiasts. The main exception to this trend came in historical writing on classical sports, notably in E. Norman Gardiner's early twentieth-century work on Greece and Rome.[12] However, the discipline of history changed and broadened so much during the twentieth century that sport belatedly fell within its remit. What changes took place to allow this to happen? To see sports history in the context of history as a whole – to see, for example, why sports history is taught at universities and seen as a legitimate area for PhD theses and academic books in the 2000s, but was not in the 1950s – we have to look at the acceptance of sport by what John Lowerson calls 'the old historical mainstream'.[13] Many strands can be teased out to see how, why, and when history as a discipline became more comprehensive in its range, and good accounts of these strands can be found in various historiography books.[14] For our purposes, the first key movement was the French-based *Annales* school, active from the late 1920s, which advocated 'total history'. Its proponents, including Fernand Braudel, Marc Bloch, and Georges LeFebvre, worked to broaden history's attention out from politics and war, and include within its remit all aspects of social, economic, cultural, demographic, and environmental history.[15] While the first generations of *Annales* did not look at sport, they helped to redefine the subject area of history in such a way that sport could later fit in. Their emphasis on interdisciplinarity was also to provide a model for later sports historians. The second key movement for sports history was the new form of social history that emerged from the Communist Party Historians Group in the UK in the 1950s, which adopted the label of 'history from below', and from a non-Communist but parallel development in popular history in the USA. In the 1960s and 1970s, historians such as E.P. Thompson, George Rudé, Eric Hobsbawm, and Rodney Hilton focused on the historical experiences of people and groups who were usually ignored or marginalised by history, such as industrial and agricultural labourers, and members of popular political and religious movements. Thompson's seminal *The Making of the English Working Class* of 1963 is widely seen as the key text of this movement, with its explicit agenda of seeking to study minority groups and overlooked people, and 'rescue [them] . . . from the enormous condescension of posterity'.[16] Lowerson has underlined this book's importance to sports history by claiming that 'almost all major British work in the field [of sports history] . . . counts as an offspring' of Thompson.[17] As with *Annales*, sport did not figure in the early work of this group of historians: their interests were more political and economic. However, the influence of this approach, particularly when applied to the leisure time pursuits and popular culture of any group from the past, was crucial in forming the template for sports history.

Annales and history from below did not, then, invent academic sports history: but they helped redefine what academic historians could study, and to revise historical research methodologies in such a way as to facilitate sports history. They set the templates in both social and cultural history (in their widest senses) into which sport could easily fit when historians chose to look at it. By the late 1960s and early 1970s, there had been enough of a change in the discipline of history – also influenced both by the demographics of higher education teaching and by changes in western societies as a whole – for historians to start tackling sport. The early sports historians attempted to tackle sport both in its own right as an activity and for the light it could shed on other areas of a society's life, such as religion, gender and class relations, economic activity, and education. It was the emphasis on contexts and connections learnt from *Annales*, and the validity of prioritising the experiences of working people that came from the history from below movement, that set the early sports historians apart from the antiquarian forerunners explored above. Dennis Brailsford, for example, linked sport and physical education to the religious and political currents of the early modern English society; J.A. Mangan firmly placed sport in the context of Victorian and Edwardian education; while Tony Mason looked at football as a part of working-class culture and urban life in the same period.[18] Aside from their great merit as studies in sports history, these pioneering books are excellent case studies in the development of a new form of historiography out of diverse influences.

3.2.3 Physical Education

Alongside this development of a more inclusive academic history, which has to be seen in context as part of the educational expansion that went with the growth of mass welfare societies after the Second World War, sports history had another disciplinary parent: physical education. The physical education and coaching professions have always been aware of their own historical development, particularly as a way of seeing how things used to be done and how and why they changed. Many coaching manuals and PE texts contain sections on the history of their particular discipline, evidence that the teachers and coaches have been keen not to reinvent the wheel, and have been happy openly to learn from history and to teach new generations of teachers and coaches the value of this approach. This approach produced some classic works of history, such as Fred Leonard's *A Guide to the History of Physical Education* and Peter McIntosh's *Physical Education in England since 1800.*[19] Sports scientists can recognise the value of studying how sports were coached in the past by thinking about how their knowledge of such issues as warm-up, recovery, and nutrition are based on experience acquired over generations. It is unlikely that a contemporary long-distance swimmer would drink beer and brandy during an event now, like Matthew Webb did during his pioneering crossing of the English Channel in 1875.[20] However, the fact that we can look at his diet historically has been helpful in getting people to move towards more efficient nutrition. This is just one example of the sense of precedent and experience from within physical education that has become a storehouse of professional knowledge, and a record of evolution. Physical education expanded in the 1960s and 1970s, again under the influence of wider educational and social change, and in response to the enhanced political profile that sport was enjoying through state patronage and health promotion. Part of this expansion was physical education's academic growth, a growth that by the 1990s had effectively invented Sport(s) Studies as a discipline in higher education. The presence of historical perspectives on sport within this discipline, along with scientific and pedagogical perspectives, helped to foster the growth of sports history. Indeed, this growth has meant that far from being exclusively a part of the history establishment explored above, sports history is also a part of the sports studies establishment. This factor has brought in the influences of sports and education departments and their respective professional networks.

3.2.4 Sociology

The next clear influence on the growth of an academically rigorous sports history came from another discipline: sociology. History and sociology have different focus points, respectively the past and the present. However, sociology as it emerged during the late nineteenth century could not help but have an interest in the past: any attempt to understand a society that does not acknowledge development over time will inevitably be lacking in perspective. In return, social historians from the early twentieth century learnt from the ways in which sociology was studying and explaining society, and picked up models and terminology (class, stratification, structures) that they could apply to past societies. There may be differences in how historians and sociologists view the past, but there has always been fruitful overlapping between practitioners in the two disciplines. For our current purposes, the interest shown in sport by some sociologists from the 1960s onwards helped to create an academic agenda for dealing with sport in society. German-born figurational sociologist Norbert Elias embraced sport within his long-term concerns with civilisation and social behaviour, while a new generation of sociologists, such as Eric Dunning and Anthony Giddens – both of whom wrote research degrees on sport in the 1960s – made sport a central theme. In the UK, key work was done here at the University of Leicester, particularly through the work of Elias and Dunning. Their emphasis on configurations stressed the importance of the past as a factor in explaining contemporary social relationships; and their interest in the civilising process created a sociology that was interested in how leisure pursuits and cultural activities contributed towards different societies' sense of identity and social standards. Sport fitted into this agenda, whether in the form of royal hunting, or the emergence of distinctive team games in modern industrial society. Dunning's edited collection of readings from 1970, *The Sociology of Sport*, contained some essays that linked past and present; and Dunning and Kenneth Sheard's *Barbarians, Gentlemen and Players*, a 1979 study of the growth of rugby football,[21] was seminal here in linking sociology and history. So too was the University of Leicester's sociologists' subsequent work on football hooliganism, such as *The Roots of Football Hooliganism*.[22] Since then, there has been a significant body of sports sociology that has been keen to avoid the approach that has 'nodded in tokenistic fashion in the direction of the historical'.[23] This historical sociology of sport has been subject to criticism from some historians for the ways in which it uses primary sources, and for the present-centred assumptions it often makes. An interesting case study here can be found in Tony Collins' critical analysis of the historical methodologies used in some of the work on sport and the civilising process.[24]

Bringing these academic strands together, we can see that the disciplines of history, physical education, and sociology all developed in such a way as to make the serious academic study of sports history possible. These changes within the disciplines put sport on the agenda, and provided historians with the training and skills to look at sport in the past. However, what comes into the territory of the historian at any time is not just governed by values and interests within the discipline. As we saw above in relation to the recent growth of history of disease, contemporary events influence the historian's agenda. What was happening in sport in the second half of the twentieth century to make historians take notice of it?

3.2.5 Sport in crisis

As we discussed during the warm-up exercises, sport has always had both positive and negative features. For every story of health improvement, there is an injury or fatality; for every sporting event that brings people together, there are events that reinforce divisions. These trends are evident in every society in history for which we have records of sport being played. However, when modern sports developed in the UK and elsewhere during the eighteenth and nineteenth centuries, they acquired certain ideological values from their promoters, players, patrons, and reporters. Qualities such as amateurism, fair play, gentlemanly conduct, and respect for the rules became part of the fabric of many sports, qualities that were reinforced by the ways in which such places as schools, universities, churches and chapels, and workplaces promoted sport. Without attempting to simplify a complex process, modern sport came to be associated with these characteristics. The negative features remained. Gambling, violence, cheating, and other supposed vices never died out, but they became the subject of condemnation, and phrases such as 'sportsmanlike', 'sporting', 'fair play', and 'playing the game' came to have resonance away from sport as markers of good behaviour. However, in the period after the Second World War, the global growth of sport and its increased commercial and political importance created a setting in which such values became less relevant. There are many markers we could use to show the cultural changes going on in sport during this period, but a few examples will have to suffice. The Olympic Games and rugby union became professionalised, governments and non-governmental political organisations became increasingly prepared to use sport to promote their causes, cheating and gamesmanship – particularly through drugs and through openly disputing officials' decisions – became more prominent, and violence around some sporting events led to social order problems. These examples are not given to try and create the idea that there was ever a golden age in sport: as we saw in Chapter 2, such an idea is highly problematic. They are given simply to show that sport's global and commercial success has created a culture in which the British middle-class values of modern sport's birth are no longer widely respected.

Where history comes in here is that just as sports history was becoming academically possible and even respectable, sport itself was becoming – at least in the public perception – increasingly problematic. This helped to set agendas for historians wanting to know how sport had developed in such ways. Sport as a whole was raising questions about itself. Whose values do the rules represent? Why have political agencies got involved? Why has a cheating culture grown? Why are some people making increasing amounts of money out of sport? Such questions can be answered only through an enquiry that starts with the past – in other words, through history. Some sports historians have been explicit about the past/present links, and how contemporary issues inspired them to go to the past. In his 1981 study of Olympic founder Pierre de Coubertin, John MacAloon drew parallels between the reality of Olympism at the time of writing and the polemics of its early days:

> I felt compelled to understand how on earth someone came to the extraordinary idea that a group of people running around in short pants every four years had something to do with international understanding and world peace.[25]

In a similar vein, Tony Collins, writing after rugby union's acceptance of professionalism in 1995 and rugby league's switch to a media-driven summer calendar, begins his *Rugby's Great Split* of 1998 with the question 'Why are there two forms of rugby?', and goes on to note that 'given the profound changes which both rugby league and rugby union are currently undergoing, the question now has an importance which transcends mere historical curiosity'.[26] These are just two examples, and they mark out the texts as products of their time. Careful reading of sports historians' work, particularly in the prefaces or introductions to their books, can provide you with evidence of how what was going on in sport, just as much as what was going on in university history departments, directed historians in particular ways. Douglas Booth calls for more of this 'reflexive historical practice',[27] and looks forward to historians recognising how their position in time has affected their approaches to the subject.

Activity 2: Questions about the past that are formed in the present

Some historians are explicit in drawing their readers' attention to the ways in which issues in the present attracted them to certain parts of sports history. The following extracts both illustrate this. In each case, look at the date of publication, then analyse the text for evidence that the piece was written at that time.

Adrian Harvey, *Football: The First Hundred Years* (2005)

> Both the varieties of football that originally hailed from Britain, the Rugby and Association games, have probably never been as popular as they are now. The association game, or soccer as it has become generally known, is now almost globally popular and judging by the last few World Cups, before long a team from Asia, Africa or North America will go on to win the trophy. Rugby's progress has been less dramatic but the game is becoming increasingly international and is surely destined to continue to expand. Of course, periodically it is likely that both varieties of football will be afflicted by problems stemming from a downturn in the world economy and difficulties generated by financial mismanagement. Collectively, however, their future appears bright. Peculiarly enough, despite this very little is known about the origins of modern football and many questions relating to its growth and development remain unanswered.[28]

Ramachandra Guha, *A Corner of a Foreign Field: The Indian History of a British Sport* (2002).

> The commercialization of modern cricket and the corruptions that have come in its wake have led some commentators to speak wistfully of a time when this was a 'gentleman's game'. In truth, there was no golden age, no uncontaminated past in which the playground was free of social pressure and social influence. Cricket has always been a microcosm of the fissures and tensions within Indian society: fissures that it both reflected and played upon, mitigated as well as intensified. The cricketer or cricket lover might seek to keep his game pure, but the historian finds himself

----

straying, willy-nilly, into those great, overarching themes of Indian history: race, caste, religion and nation.[29]

Read the prefaces and introductions of all the history books that you use, and try to make similar connections of your own. Remember to look carefully at the date of publication to know what 'contemporary' means for them. What are the implications for your philosophy of history of this kind of approach?

3.2.6 The scope of sports history

Bringing these themes together, we could end up thinking that all history is really about the present, and that all history books are simply historians' autobiographies. I am not making that claim: the subject matter remains the past, and this is what distinguishes history from other disciplines, however much interdisciplinarity we practise with our colleagues in sociology, physical education, education, and other areas. The point of this section has been to demonstrate that a new branch of history, such as sports history, does not just happen. It emerges when the academic environment encourages it, when the subject matter itself is deemed interesting and worthy of study, and when contemporary issues in sport push people into looking for explanations in the past.

These developments have given us the multifaceted sports history that we now enjoy, and it is important to appreciate this diversity if we hope to make sense of the different traditions evident in the different history we read. First, we have academic sports history in its own right, a type of historiography that you will find in monographs, textbooks, and journal articles written by specialists whose main teaching and research is in the area of sport. This type of sports history is supported by an infrastructure of university courses, journals (such as *The International Journal of the History of Sport*, *Sport in History*, *The Journal of Sport History*, and *Sporting Traditions*), societies and associations (such as the International Society for the History of Physical Education and Sport, the British Society of Sports History, and the North American Society of Sport History), and specialist series by various publishing houses (such as Routledge's *Sport in the Global Society* and the University of Illinois' *Sport and Society* series). The next aspect is in the growing recognition by non-sports historians of sport's relevance, and their consequent inclusion of sport in more mainstream texts. Arthur Marwick, Eric Hobsbawm, Asa Briggs, and many others have used sport to illustrate trends in the societies under discussion. Keith Robbins, for example, placed sport alongside religion and education in his section on 'the battle for minds and bodies' in early twentieth-century Britain in his *The Eclipse of a Great Power* of 1983, while political historian Kenneth Morgan included examples from football for his survey of the 1960s in *The People's Peace* of 1990.[30] Non-sports-based journals have increasingly included articles on sports history, such as *Contemporary British History*'s special edition on professionalism and amateurism in sport,[31] and have reviewed sports history books, a clear recognition of sport history's growing respectability and relevance. Similarly, series of books on particular aspects of history, or approaches to it, increasingly include sports titles, such as Holt's *Sport and the British* in Oxford University Press's *Oxford Studies in Social History*, Scott Simon's *Jackie Robinson and the Integration of Baseball* in Wiley's *The Turning Point* series, or David McComb's *Sports in World History* in Routledge's *Themes in World History* series.[32] Many authors continue to provide high-quality narrative history of particular sporting events, such as William Fotheringham on the Tour de France, Eliot Asinof on the World Series, and Simon Reeve on the 1972 Olympics.[33] Sporting biography remains a popular genre, with recent examples such as Simon Rae's *W.G. Grace* and David Remnick's study of Muhammad Ali, *King of the World*.[34] History from the point of view of fans and enthusiasts has had a new lease of life since the 1992 publication of Nick Hornby's *Fever Pitch*, with many authors interweaving their own involvement with narratives of wider historical events. This has gone beyond football, and sports as diverse as greyhound racing, swimming, scuba diving, and fell-running have been the subject of this kind of attention.[35] The Internet has helped this development, as it allows people to disseminate their stories without the traditional constraints of the publishing industry. Not all of this material is reliable, and you should read all of it critically, but there are plenty of high-quality sites offering historical statistics, anecdotes, and discussions, including RL1908 on Australian rugby league, Baseball Almanac, and soccerbase.[36] This list of different types of literature, with examples, is designed to identify the many different forms that sports history writing now takes. We shall be looking at the character of some of these types, and what you can get out of them, in Chapter 4: for now, simply recognise the range of literature that exists.

► **3.3 Contemporary sports history as a product of its past**

So, the study of sports history cannot be seen out of the context of its disciplinary and academic background. How have these circumstances of sports history's own evolution influenced the discipline? Just as you might note a family resemblance between a mother and her child, you can look for ways in which a discipline's current shape is influenced by its parentage. What follows is an attempt to see how sports history's parentage is evident in its current appearance. It is not an exhaustive survey. History as whole, and sports history as part of it, moves far too quickly to be pinned down in such a way. However, it is a useful exercise, and a logical conclusion to this chapter, to see some of the ways in which contemporary sports history is recognisable as the product of the factors we have explored above.

3.3.1 Stratification and minority groups

First, we can see that sports history has always been, and remains, concerned with social stratification. The legacy of history from below embedded social class as a concern of sports history from its start. Class runs through the pioneering work of Tony Mason, Richard Gruneau, Richard Holt, Stephen Jones, Wray Vamplew, and J.A. Mangan, with sports from various historical periods being explored in terms of how different social groups invested their physical activities with markers of community, identity, and exclusivity. Class has remained a constant theme in many national traditions of sports history.[37] Its analysis has gone beyond the predominantly economic concerns of early Marxism, with many sports historians engaging with the more nuanced and subtle cultural Marxism associated with Antonio Gramsci's work. Here, historians analysed the power relations in the societies they were studying, looking at the ways in which different power groups (classes, genders, ethnic groups, religious denominations, and so on) maintained power through culture as well as coercion.[38] This emphasis on class has been most obvious in any sports history text that deals with social class in problematic terms. A lot of this work is explicitly focused on the working-class experience. Jones' monographs on working-class sport and leisure are good examples of this. In *Workers at Play* and *Sport, Politics and the Working Class*, he explored the themes of working-class identity, economic activity, and political activism through their experiences in the area of sport and leisure.[39] A more theoretical work was John Hargreaves' 1986 *Sport, Power and Culture*, which set out its approach early on:

> We are … not so much concerned with giving a comprehensive account of sport as such … but with understanding the way in which sports as cultural formations may, in certain respects, be connected with the power apparatus.[40]

Sports history's roots in the history from below movement have also influenced its interests in other forms of stratification and power relations. In particular, gender, ethnicity, and nationality have become solid themes in their own right. Various historians and historically minded sociologists have looked at the ways in which the same markers that concerned the class-conscious first generation – inclusion and exclusion, the exercise of power, the links between play and identity – have also been evident along gender,[41] ethnic[42] and national lines.[43] Taken together, sports history's concern with the ways in which sports have developed along lines of stratification that exist in wider society and how those lines have influenced such aspects of sport as accessibility, physical location, rules, etiquette, and popularity are part of its inheritance from history from below.

3.3.2 Education

If sports history has learnt about stratification from its Marxist roots, then its interest in education has come from the PE side of its family tree. Seminal early texts, such as Brailsford's *Sport and Society: Elizabeth to Anne*, and their emphasis on the role of sport and physical recreation as historical teaching tools helped to identify the role of education.[44] Mangan's influential work on private schools, *Athleticism in the Victorian and Edwardian Public School*, took this interest a step further, providing not just a framework for how modern sports owed a significant part of their development to Victorian scholastic enthusiasm, but also a detailed case study of the links that existed between educational philosophy and organised physical activity in a discreet period of history.[45] Studies of Victorian scholastic sport have remained a popular staple of British sports history, a staple reinforced by the emphasis given to this period of sport's development by university and A-level courses. Other areas of educational sport have not been as attractive to historians: sport and physical education in the state sector and university sport have been relatively neglected. However, the centrality of the nineteenth-century educational initiatives in sports historiography has been forged, in part, from the PE roots of sports history.

3.3.3 Theoretical perspectives

Finally, sports history's lines of evolution can be seen in its sometimes ambivalent attitude towards theoretical movements in history. 'Theory' can be an off-putting word, so it is worth breaking it down. It has a number of meanings, depending on the exact context, but what they all have in common is their emphasis on mental, abstract, and speculative aspects. The most relevant model for us is to see a theory as a system or a plan devised by an observer to explain a phenomenon, a plan which becomes 'the framework of interpretation'[46] of that phenomenon. The phenomenon may be social, historical, philosophical, or anything else, depending on the field in which the observer is working – every academic discipline, from anthropology to zoology, has theorists, although the role of theory is stronger in some subjects, such as literary studies and mathematics, than in others, including history. In these fields, theorists use their theories to create models of behaviour, to explain occurrences, and sometimes to predict the future. There is always a link between theory and practice, with even the most committed theorists basing their work on detailed analyses of their more practical colleagues' applied work. Theory thus becomes a way of looking at the world, a way of explaining things.

When we come to history, it is clear that theory is a problematic subject.[47] Many historians have used theories in the sense outlined above, as Tosh's 'framework of interpretation'. They have used different theoretical perspectives, such as Marxism, feminism, post-colonialism, and post-modernism, as lenses through which to study the past, and have drawn their methods and research questions from particular theoretical traditions. There are many advantages to this approach. The human past is so huge that we need some way of navigating through it, and a clearly defined set of questions can serve that purpose. Theories can help us to focus, and to organise our material into manageable chunks. They can add critical weight to our findings, and give them a structure. Whereas history writing without a theoretical perspective can be disorganised and anecdotal, that which is underpinned by a clear theory can be coherent and structured. However, many historians are also wary of theory, seeing it as a threat. In this view, theories are abstract constructs developed in the present. They might help to explain general trends, but they are inadequate in dealing with what sports historian Richard Holt calls 'complex historical reality'.[48] In this rather sceptical view, theories are mistrusted because they make historians look only for the evidence that will help them make their point: two historians from different theoretical perspectives could look at the same material and come up with wholly contradictory results.

This is far more than a debate about sports history: historical philosophers and authors of general methodology and historiography texts have long argued over this issue. Arthur Marwick summed up the divisions well:

> There are those... who feel that without a body of theory history cannot claim to be regarded as a respectable academic subject....Yet, the simple indisputable fact remains that practising historians as a profession are united neither in the acceptance of one body of theory, not even in the view that theoretical approaches are helpful or desirable.[49]

The latter group of historians cited in this quotation, the theoretical sceptics, have many supporters amongst students. Theoretical perspectives, when introduced to historical study, are often resisted by students on various grounds. Some share Holt's view, and find theories as inadequate to deal with the infinite possibilities of what happened in the past. Others reject them on grounds of language, finding their jargon to be unhelpful; or they are seen as too dogmatically linked to particular contemporary ideologies – such as Marxism or feminism – to be of use in dealing with periods where different world views dominated. Sometimes the resistance is based on nothing more than an antipathy towards anything that tries to over-complicate and over-intellectualise sport.

Within sports history, there has long been what John Horne, Alan Tomlinson, and Garry Whannel call a 'creative tension'[50] between those with an overly empirical outlook and those who have sought to bring in theoretical perspectives, and there remains a powerful strand of empiricism in much sports history. Such basic questions as 'what happened?' and 'why did it happen?', as well as the building blocks of history that are labelled 'when?', 'who?', 'how?', and 'where?', are all driven by the empiricist assumption that we can find clear answers if we look hard enough at all the evidence, regardless of any theory. Documentary analysis of appropriate primary evidence has been a constant base for sports history research, and in most popular sports, historians – those working on club or organisational records, for example – evidently view their task as recovering what happened in the past and presenting it for readers as the definitive account. The 'complete history' culture, dominated by detailed records of players, matches, seasons, and statistics, is pure empiricism. Where this approach is limited for academics, of course, is in the authors' failure to question their approach, or to appreciate the inherent subjectivities involved in writing official or aligned history. We can also see empiricist beliefs at work whenever sports historians use language that assumes comprehensive coverage, most obviously when an author chooses to use the definite 'The history of . . . ' rather than the indefinite 'A history of . . . '

▶ **3.4 Conclusion**

This chapter has aimed to give you an overview of the relationship between history as an academic discipline and sport as a subject matter. It has introduced the key factors that have encouraged historians to take sport seriously, and given you some examples through which you can see these factors at work. It should also have opened up further areas for enquiry for you. Through this, you should now have a grasp of the disciplinary roots of sports history, and a sense of perspective on the books and articles you read, and the courses you study. You should also have a sense of sports history's interrelationship with history and sports studies as bigger disciplines. You now need to apply this material to everything that you read, and to the ways in which you write about sports history. Your work will increase in sophistication if it contains historiographical awareness: so take the ideas from this chapter and connect them with your own research.

4 Reading Sports History

If you have not read much history before, then starting on a sports history text can be a strange experience, just as a historian without a scientific background might flounder when faced with a biomechanics textbook. Building on the discussions of the nature of history, the dimensions of sports historiography, and the role of theory in sports history, this chapter aims to provide some practical guidance on using sports history texts. It introduces the main types of sports history text that you will come across, and provides some critical commentary on the nature of each type. It also provides examples. The range of sources covered here includes both academic and popular sports history, a distinction that needs to be made to help you recognise the nature of any source you use. The unifying factor here is that we are looking at secondary sources: things that have been created after the events that you are studying, and which are dependent on evidence from the time that you are studying. 'Secondary' here does not mean inferior or less significant than primary: it is simply a question of timing and orientation. This chapter aims to introduce you to the range of secondary sources that is available to you, and to get you asking critical questions about every text that you use.

▶ 4.1 Approaching secondary sources

We have already looked at some of the ways in which historians' writings are relative to the time in which they work. As well as the philosophical and cultural reasons for this, it is important not to overlook a basic factor in relative historiography: that historians can work only in the media that are available to them, and produce different kinds of work that are possible in those media. For example, a nineteenth-century historian such as Thomas Macaulay could publish only in books or periodicals, whereas a contemporary historian such as Simon Schama has such options as television, radio, and the Internet available as well as the older media. The first point to stress, then, in relation to using historians' work is that you need to think historically and contextually about the nature of each text. What forms were available to the historian at the time? Why did he or she choose to use a particular media? What constraints and opportunities exist within each medium? Beyond this, you need to consider the specific nature of any medium in which sports historians work, and to be able to identify the nature of every type of source. This involves you in thinking about such issues as any given text's remit, its intended audience, and the ways in which it relates to other sources.

Beyond this, you need to get into the habit of asking historiographical questions about any text, which involves applying the kind of themes raised in previous chapters to all of the texts that you use. When was it written? Who wrote it? Where was it written? What has its publishing history been? What was going on in sport at the time that might have influenced the author? Questions of this type can help you avoid basic errors. For example, a British text referring to the impact of the Civil War on sport will be looking at the mid-seventeenth century, whereas an American text using the words 'Civil War' will be looking two centuries later. This line of questioning can also help you to put each text in its own context, and so avoid making anachronistic judgements about them. For example, the first edition of Eric Dunning and Kenneth Sheard's historical analysis of rugby union, *Barbarians, Gentlemen and Players*, was published in 1979, a time when the sport was still fervently amateur. Its second edition came out in 2004, 9 years after the sport accepted professionalism. To use either edition without noticing its date of publication, and linking those dates to the book's content and conclusions, would be to miss the chance to appreciate historiography in action.[1]

The categories of text that I have chosen are designed to cover as wide a range of sports history as possible. They are also designed to encourage you to think and read across the academic/non-academic boundaries identified in Chapter 3, and to look at the ways in which sports historians engage with the theoretical perspectives. Through this, you are encouraged to analyse the nature of every text you use, and not simply to take them for granted. Think about each text's nature, remit, audience, and aims, and look at it in the wide context of historiography. The aim is to help you get the most out of everything you read, and to help you become more reflective and critical as a historian than you can be if you simply read the text as some kind of objective and neutral story. This chapter is also designed to help you consider the full range of secondary resources that is available to you, and to help you choose the most suitable and most appropriate, rather than simply the most recent or most easily available. It is worth stressing that all of the genres of text that we consider are established within the wider field of history as a whole. It is thus useful to think of them both as history texts that deal with sport and as sports texts that deal with history. Moreover, you need to remember that in the UK, most sports historians' disciplinary affiliations are, on the whole, with history, although in some other countries there are stronger links between sports science and sports history. However, wherever the disciplinary links are, sports historians tend to have more in common methodologically and pedagogically with, say, military historians than with sports physiologists. Similarly, a sports history journal article has far more in common – structurally, methodologically, stylistically – with a history journal article on a non-sporting theme than it does with a sports science journal article.

Activity 1: Sports history texts and their wider disciplinary affiliations

In order to enhance your understanding of the disciplinary traditions within which history texts work, carry out a comparative study of the following types of journal article:

- *A sports history article from one of the following journals* International Journal of the History of Sport, Sport in History, Journal of Sports History, Sport History Review, Sporting Traditions.

- *A history article about anything other than sport from one of the following journals* Modern History Review, English Historical Review, American Historical Journal, Journal of Contemporary History, Australian Historical Studies, Canadian Journal of History.

- *A sports science article from one of the following journals* European Journal of Sport Science, International Journal of Sport Nutrition, Journal of Applied Sport Psychology, Sport Science Review.

Look for the following features of each article:

- overall structure and use of section headings

- length

- style of referencing

- writing style and language

- use of quoted or cited material from other published sources

- use of primary evidence/data.

Now answer the following questions:

1. What does the sports history article have in common with each of the other articles?

2. In what ways does it differ from the other articles?

3. At whom is each article aimed? Who are the assumed audiences? How can you work this out?

4. How much grounding in the discipline does the author assume his or her readers to have?

With this exercise in mind, we can move on now to consider the main types of secondary source that you will use as a sports history student. The key point to remember when dealing with them all is based on the old sporting proverb 'horses for courses'. In sports history, as in any other subject, no single text will tell you all you need to know, and reliance on only one type of source will limit the breadth and the depth of your knowledge. It will also limit your critical engagement with the subject: seeing what expert academics, teachers, and a club's own historians say about the same event will help you get a sense of how contested history is, and how different people have different perspectives on it. Think back to the discussion of myths and the 'invention of tradition' in Chapter 2: using a governing body's own website may be of limited use if you want to read analytical historical material about the sport's origin, but it will be fruitful for your research on the sport's view of itself and its own culture and history. If you read only from one of these angles, you will miss a lot, and may well not pick up on debates and controversies. So think about the type of sources you are using, and try to balance genres.

▶ 4.2 Different types of sports history texts

To work effectively as a sports historian, you need to be able to identify the different types of text that historians produce. This ability serves the practical purpose of helping you read and take notes quickly and effectively: if you know what to expect from a text book or a monograph, for example, your use of them will be far more effective than if you go to them unreflectively assuming that you have to read every word and that you will then have all the answers. The main types of secondary you are likely to use are as follows.[2]

4.2.1 Textbook

A textbook is a book that has been produced specifically to cater for the demands of a particular syllabus or curriculum. It is structured in a way that reflects the content and order of the curriculum, and is directed almost exclusively at a readership of people taking that course. Authors will generally be teachers and/or lecturers in the field, who have direct experience of teaching the course. Typically, a textbook will go through numerous editions, with the authors revising it on a regular basis so that the material remains current, and so that publishers can maximise sales by reducing the second-hand market. An example is *Physical Education and the Study of Sport* by Bob Davis, Ros Bull, Jan Roscoe, and Dennis Roscoe.[3]

4.2.2 Work of synthesis

A synthesis is something that brings together a variety of sources. For historians, a work of synthesis is a book that brings together original research from a variety of other authors, and presents it in an accessible, digestible form. Often combining thematic and chronological approaches, the synthesis is not as closely tied to a curriculum as a textbook, and is likely to have a more analytical approach. A sports history example is Jeffrey Hill's *Sport, Leisure and Culture in Twentieth-Century Britain*.[4]

4.2.3 Monograph

A monograph is a specialised book based on extensive primary research. As Black and MacRaild point out, monographs are often 'born out of PhD...theses, rewritten, broadened out and published because they offer a new argument or a fresh look at old problems'.[5] For undergraduates working on multidisciplinary sports courses, history monographs can be daunting, as they require you to understand many of the traditions and protocols of historical writing: whereas the author of a textbook will be aiming at you as an undergraduate, the author of a monograph is aiming at a smaller and more specialised audience of peers. However, this does not mean that you should ignore them: the opposite is true. Most of the dynamic and pioneering work in sports history goes on in monographs. Examples include Peter Beck's *Scoring for Britain*, David Young's *The Modern Olympics*, and Greg Ryan's *The Making of New Zealand Cricket.*[6]

4.2.4 Edited collection

This is an edited book on a particular theme, in which the editors commission new essays from various other authors. Typically, it will have an editor's introduction, with the rest of the book given over to the individual authors' chapters. Some that will be relevant to you cover far more than just sports history. In sports studies, for example, Eric Dunning and Jay Coakley's *Handbook of Sports Studies* and Barrie Houlihan's *Sport and Society: A Student Introduction* both contain numerous essays on social, cultural, and historical aspects of sport that will help your sports history work.[7] Some edited collections are specifically on a theme in sports history, such as Donald Spivey's *Sport in America* and Adrian Smith and Dilwyn Porter's *Sport and National Identity in the Post-War World.*[8] Moreover, in line with the developments discussed in Chapter 3 about mainstream history taking sport seriously, some collections on wider historical themes contain sports history essays, such as Tony Mason's chapter on sport in Paul Johnson's book on twentieth-century British history.[9]

4.2.5 Academic journal article

An academic journal is a regular periodical (published two, three, or four times a year) devoted to a particular academic theme or subject area. It publishes original research, usually in the form of long articles (anything from 6000 to 10,000 words each), as well as short articles, book reviews, and review essays. In addition, some journals carry such features as notes on research in progress and obituaries of prominent figures in the field. Journal articles are always peer-reviewed, with items submitted being scrutinised by other academics as well as editors before they are published. In sports history, key journals include *International Journal of the History of Sport*, *Sporting Traditions*, *Journal of Sport History*, and *Sport in History*. Other journals – both in general history and in other areas of sports studies – also carry sports history articles. For example, the *Journal of Contemporary History* is a non-sports history journal that sometimes includes sports-based articles, while *Sociology of Sport Journal* has carried some essentially historical material. A number of academic journals are available both in hard copy and in online versions, while some, such as *SOSOL*, are exclusively online.[10] All university libraries carry a sample of journals, with their selections tied to the curriculum of that university's courses; and you can easily get articles from journals that your university does not take, through inter-library loans systems or through the Internet. For example, the Amateur Athletic Foundation of Los Angeles (AAFLA) carries a huge supply of free articles from such journals as *Sporting Traditions* and *Sport in History* on its digital archive.[11] Journal articles are important for sports history, particularly in their provision of short and relatively accessible ways into the reading and debates on a particular issue, and they offer a good introduction to how primary historical research can be designed and written up. Indeed, if you are thinking of doing a dissertation in sports history, then you would do well to view a journal article as something of a template.

4.2.6 Website

A website is a resource that exists only on the Internet (as opposed to, for example, sources from the categories above which may be available electronically, such as e-books, as well as in hard published copies). The bulk of sports history websites are not academic in origin, tending to be produced by organisations (such as clubs and governing bodies) or individual enthusiasts. Examples of the kind of sites you might come across include the history sections of clubs' and organisations' official websites, such as the history section of the International Olympic Committee's site, or an enthusiast-based site, such as the sports-related entries in Wikipedia.[12] As with any source, you need to ask careful questions of any website you use, and you need to remember that the quality controls that exist in the academic book and journal publishing industry based on scholarly editing and peer review do not take place on the majority of websites. However, this does not mean that you should avoid using the Web. Whereas Web resources may often be unsuitable under the disciplinary criteria of sports science, their popular and inherently opinionated nature makes them ideal for sports history research, as long as you remain critical and reflective on those opinions. They can tell us a great deal about the mentality, perceptions, and imaginations of sports enthusiasts, and about what the past of their sport means to them. They can also give us access to conversations about the past through discussion boards and chat rooms, conversations with which we can join.

4.2.7 Reference book

A sports history reference book is a text that is primarily concerned with the facts and figures of sport. They range from encyclopaedias, such as Richard Cox et al's *Encyclopedia of British Sport* and David Levinson and Karen Christensen's *Encyclopedia of World Sport*, through to sports-specific record books, such as David Wallechinsky's masterly *The Complete Book of the Olympics* and *Complete Book of the Winter Olympics*, both of which are updated after each Olympic Games.[13] Such books can generally be trusted to contain detailed statistics, records, and achievement lists: Wallechinsky, for example, has comprehensive coverage of every event at every modern Olympic Games since 1896, including personal details of finalists, rules and scoring systems, and details of discontinued sports. He also includes narratives and background anecdotes at many points. You should not expect such sources, however, to be thorough on analysis or contextualisation, as even when they are written and edited by the most professional historians, their remit is to provide details and facts.

4.2.8 Popular history book

The popular sports history book is one that is written primarily for a non-academic audience. They tend to deal with such things as clubs, individual players, localities, or individual sports. An hour spent in a local studies library should glean you plenty of examples from the community in which you live. Such books are usually written by enthusiastic amateurs with a direct involvement in the sport or the club concerned, and while they usually contain enormous amounts of fascinating and useful detail, they tend to lack contextual awareness: as Wray

Vamplew put it, while 'some amateurs have produced work that ranks alongside that of the best academic and professional writers...they too often deal with their topic without reference to the wider issues'.[14] Such failure to look wider can often be frustrating to readers, and make us wish for the authors to research in more general primary sources as well as those that relate only to the club in question. However, you should be prepared to use popular history as a source of detail and narrative, and to recognise that few academic historians are likely to cover individual clubs in such detail.

This list covers most of the secondary sources that you are likely to come across. You are likely to use some texts that might not fit comfortably into any of the given categories, and you should use this list as a working taxonomy rather than as a rigid classification. For example, many reference books could also be classed as popular history, while you will find examples of all of these genres on the Internet, in such areas as history sections on club websites or personal weblogs about following a sport. However, forcing yourself to think about the texts from the viewpoint assumed here – that each text is an example of a genre, and that each one will have a particular set of strengths and weaknesses for you as a historian, whatever its overall worth – will get you into the appropriate 'horses for courses' frame of mind. It should stop you from simply treating every book, website, or article as a straightforward source of information, and get you critically engaging with them instead.

▶ **4.3 Using secondary sources**

So, with the categories in place, what do you do? What should you look for when trying to read sports history? How can you use the secondary sources? The rest of this chapter is devoted to the kind of aspects that you should look for in each text if you want to get maximum benefit from it. These aspects are worth considering if you want to find out about each text's place in the wider historiography: how to put them into their relevant contexts; how to find out about their authors; and how to look at the texts as intellectual, social, and commercial products. To help you develop here, we will explore the different genres of sports historians' works through the following themes: audiences and motives; authority and expertise; publishing history; serendipity; design; and common pitfalls.

4.3.1 Audiences and motives

Why is any text written? In Chapter 1, we explored the general reasons why people engage with sports history: but how is this engagement applied? What motivates any given historian to produce any given text? Thinking about the reasons why specific texts are produced is a good way of contextualising them.

Texts are written for a variety of reasons, and, in each case, for a mixture of those reasons. Money must never be dismissed. Few academic historians of any kind earn enough from their writings to be able to make a sole living from it. However, the earnings that can be made from writing often act as a supplementary source of income for academics. From the types of source listed above, journal articles are rarely paid for, and monographs have such a specialised audience – typically, other academics and research students – that they tend to yield only small royalties. Syntheses and textbooks can be more lucrative, as they are often set as core reading on various courses, and they can be assured of decent sales amongst students and in university libraries. Chapters in edited collections will usually bring a one-off fee. Academic websites are not produced with a profit motive. Only a small number of popular sports history books are commercially viable; and the bulk of club- or community-based studies are, like monographs, written for such specialised audiences that they have to be seen as labours of love. Personal histories and autobiographies are more commercial in orientation than any of the other categories; but for every publishing success story such as *Fever Pitch* there are many more titles that fail to make an impact. However, while direct financial return in the form of royalties may not be a leading motivation, especially for sports history academics, the development of a research and publishing profile is essential in all university systems for promotion and access to research grants. Moreover, structures of educational research funding require academics to publish regularly and frequently in books and journals with academic credibility: if they do not meet certain quotas, then their institutions can lose research monies. This has had the effect of increasing the number of journals being produced in all fields, as journal articles are quicker to write than books and can thus give each academic a longer list of publications than if he or she concentrated solely on books; and sports history is no exception. So while it would be misleading to present profit and career progression as the main motivations behind the growth of sports history, it would be naive to ignore it as a factor. Publishing is an economic activity in its own right, and it is a factor in academic career structures.

A more fundamental motive can be seen as the historian's need to cater for increasing numbers of students in higher education, a trend evident in all western societies. Without this growth, and the proliferation of subjects that it has engendered, sports history would still be a minority affair with little academic credibility. Courses need texts, and textbooks and works of synthesis are written with those specific markets in mind. Any sports historian – or, indeed, any academic – proposing a book idea to a publisher needs to identify such markets, and book proposals which cannot highlight how the book could be marketed at specific groups of students are unlikely to be commissioned. It then becomes possible to see the teaching of courses and the texts that support them in an interrelationship. When you pick up any book, try to identify if such links exist for it. In the case of textbooks, this is usually obvious. A good example is Davis, Bull, Roscoe, and Roscoe's *Physical Education and the Study of Sport*, which, while not exclusively about sports history, devotes a significant space to social and historical aspects of sport. The authors' credentials show that they are heavily involved in teaching, examining, and devising these same courses, and the Preface makes the market explicit, linking the text's evolution over four editions to changes in the curriculum and the wider settings of sport and education.[15] By noting these points of any text's remit, you can begin to locate it historiographically, and so be aware of what it can offer you. In this case, as an A-level text written by experts, you can be sure of its authority, and of its relevance to a particular course of study; but it should also alert you to the fact that it is likely to lack depth for higher level study. Moreover, its comprehensive coverage of the whole A-level syllabus – 'the performer in action', 'the performer as a person', and 'the performer in a social setting' – means that sports history is only part of its remit, and so it cannot be expected to have the depth of coverage of history that you may need in higher level research. This is the kind of quick analysis that you can carry out on every text that you use, so that you can get a sense of its orientation and potential value.

Authors, then, write for a variety of reasons and a variety of audiences. Being able to identify both motivation and intended readership will help you to understand any text more fully than if you simply approach it as a source of information. Looking at dedications, prefaces, authors' backgrounds and careers, and the publisher's remit will give you access to this contextual information. We come back to this chapter's guiding proverb, 'horses for courses'. Only a few sports history texts that you use during your studies will have been written primarily for you as a student, or for your immediate purposes of getting information for an assignment. Thinking about their remit can help you appreciate this, and thus help you notice any text's limitation, constraints, and benefits.

4.3.2 Theoretical perspectives

As we saw in Chapter 3, some sports historians have remained resistant to over-theorising their work, while others have embraced theoretical perspectives. This theme is explored in some detail in Booth's *The Field*, where he broadly divides sports historians into reconstructionists, constructionists, and deconstructionists, and shows how the former 'reject theory', preferring the 'empirical investigation of particular actions, events and ideas rather than ... abstract concepts and processes'.[16] However, many other sports historians have been more explicit in their use of theoretical perspectives, and your reading of their works will be enhanced if you know what to look out for in this area. For example, historians working within the traditions of Marxism and history from below are likely to use the vocabulary of social class, and to write up their works in ways which foreground stratification, oppression, and class identity. John Hargreaves' *Sport, Power and Culture* is perhaps an extreme example of this, but it shows the trend off very well. Chapters on such themes as 'Consolidating the Bourgeois Model' and 'Sport and the Recomposition of the Working Class in Modern Britain' are clear markers to his approach.[17] Similarly, historians working on gender in sport have tended to approach the subject through the heterogeneous perspective of feminism, and have asked questions and written up their analysis in that tradition's language. This has been obvious, both in the work on women's sports history that has grown since Allen Guttmann's *Women's Sports* and Patricia Vertinsky's *The Eternally Wounded Woman*, and in the more recent critical analysis of men's sport as a gendered subject, evident in such texts as John Nauright and Timothy Chandler's *Making Men* and Varda Burstyn's *The Rites of Man*.[18] Some sports historians have embraced post-modernism as a theoretical perspective, and explored sports history in sceptical and critical terms, questioning the nature of the evidence and the structures of the narratives that historians create.[19] Examples of this approach can be seen in authors' deliberate use of caution over certainty, their emphasis on the provisional and relative nature of historical knowledge, and their explorations of discourses rather than events.

We shall be returning to some of these themes in the Conclusion: for now, the point is to help you recognise that some sports historians use particular theoretical perspectives in their work, and that the language in which they write, and the structures they place on their texts, will reflect and embody these perspectives. Careful reading of introductions, parallel reading out from the texts and into the authors' references, and a keen ear for specialised vocabulary can all help to enhance your awareness of any text's theoretical underpinning.

4.3.3 Authority and expertise

What makes you trust a historian? It is relatively easy to gauge the authority and expertise of any teacher or lecturer with whom you work. You can notice both expertise and gaps in his or her knowledge and methods in class, or in one-to-one sessions on written work. However, when you are reading the published work of people to whom you do not have direct access, it is often easy just to take it on trust and assume expertise and authority. The publishing industry relies on this assumption: nobody would buy books written by a historian with a reputation for inaccuracy; and academic books and journal articles go through quality control procedures designed to get rid of errors before publication. Mistakes can still survive into print: any honest sports historian will acknowledge at least one factual error in his or her work. However, the relationship between reader and historian is based on an assumption of trust.

So what do you look for to tell you the sports historian's credentials? First, find out about his or her professional background. Most books will contain some biographical or professional information about the author. This will usually take the form of, at least, a note of the author's academic position at the time of publication, such as 'Allen Guttmann is professor of American Studies at Amherst College' from the dust jacket of his *The Olympics*.[20] Always check dates here: the fact that the author worked at a particular institution when the book was published does not mean that he or she still works there when you are using the book. Even without this starting point, an Internet search can usually give you background information on most academics. If you know an author's current institution, then go straight to its home page; if you do not, then use a search engine to locate the author. From here, you should be able to get a fair idea of what the author's professional background is. Is he or she primarily a historian? Does he or she teach as well as research in the area? Find out about his or her other research and publications. By looking at any author's own list of publications, easily accessible through university websites, you can get a sense of how expertise and authority are developed. Look at the dates of publication: how frequently does he or she publish? Look at the range of subjects: does he or she write just sports history, or other kinds of history too? Look at the publishers: what kind of books do they publish? Find out what other historians think of his or her work by looking for reviews of the text, and for citations of the text in other publications. This is one of the best ways to check any author's expertise and status: how often, and in what way, do his or her peers and those coming afterwards use his or her work? Frequent mentions in reference lists and bibliographies, frequent quotation and citation, and formal acknowledgement can all be used as indicators. It is particularly useful to look at some non-sports history writing in this context, as it shows the extent to which sports historians have been noticed by the mainstream.

4.3.4 Publishing history

In some areas of sports studies, you will be used to the idea that only the most recent work counts. Constant development and refinement of research in the laboratory-based areas of sports science and the ever-changing legal and financial contexts for sports business and policy studies mean that it is crucial to keep up-to-date with the latest research. Historical research is similarly subject to revision, thanks to the constant development of methodologies, the availability of new sources, and the impact of new theories and ideologies on research. As new historical material becomes available, so new research can be done that adds to the historiography: think, for example, of the ways in which the history of British sports diplomacy will be revisited and revised in 2011, when the government's files on the 1980 Moscow Olympic boycott will be released. And, as we have seen in an earlier chapter, new areas of study are consistently coming to light. So, just as the authors of scientific and business-based materials revise and update their works, so do sports historians. Revisions can range from such minor aspects as the correction of errors right through to the inclusion of new material and the wholesale rewriting of a section to cater for new readerships. Revision also happens in new editions of monographs, where changing times and attitudes will be reflected – and, indeed, embodied – in the text. Dunning and Sheard's *Barbarians, Gentlemen and Players* was first published in 1979. Its second edition, published in 2004, provided detail and analysis on the changes that had occurred in rugby union since the late 1970s, including the acceptance of professionalism and the growth of global competition.[21] To track such changes, look out for the books' titles themselves: the use of such key words as 'revisited' or 'revised' suggests that the subject matter has been rethought. You can also follow changes by looking at the chapter titles and the book's structure, the additional sources used, the ways in which new literature is covered, the introductory material, and the acknowledgements, which can provide evidence of the changing academic context. You should thus see new editions not just as attempts to bring history up to date, but also as an exercise in revisiting the events of the past in the light of the concerns of the present. The relative nature of historiography is never clearer than when we compare editions of a book.

4.3.5 Serendipity

Serendipity is the act of finding something when you are looking for something else. Academically, it is a useful aspect of any reading; and the fact that it happens is welcome evidence of the subjective and unpredictable nature of any study. For example, when flicking through a journal to find an article that you are seeking, you may come across a book review on a related subject, or the obituary of a prominent academic, or a call for papers for a conference in the area you are researching. This sort of accidental research happens in sports history, as in any other branch of study; but it can happen only if you approach your reading with an open mind that allows you to notice the potential of unexpected things, and with the open eyes and ears that I explored in the warm-up exercises. For it to work, you need to be attuned to the kind of words and phrases that might be of interest. The Internet has expanded our opportunities for serendipity exponentially, particularly when we surf or use portals and gateways to access information. Even within a single site, the opportunities are great: think of the way in which the digital archive at AAFLA allows you to jump from academic journal articles on many aspects of sports history to the official reports of all of the modern Olympic Games in seconds. However, serendipity has its dangers: it can encourage us to waste time on peripheral issues instead of concentrating on our remit at any given time. You need to retain both discipline over your study time and order over your notes if you are to use serendipity to your advantage.

4.3.6 Design

Like many of the features of sport that we take for granted, such as rules and timing, the design and layout of secondary sources is something that we often fail to reflect upon. In common sense terms, a book is a book, an article is an article, and a website is a website. However, reflecting on such aspects of a source as its typeface (font), layout, relationships between text and images, and the length of separate sections can tell us a great deal about the author's intentions and the targeted audience. Consideration of these features can also give us historiographical information about the time and the place of publication. This is another way in which you as a sports historian can get beneath the skin of any text you use, and thus get more out of it. For example, compare a text-heavy monograph with a popular reference work, which is likely to have pictures on every page, many tables and charts giving results and statistics, and relatively few blocks of text. Look at the way in which source material is presented in each case. The monograph will present it in conventional academic ways, through the use of one of the standard referencing systems, and will provide a reference for every quotation and citation; while the popular text is likely to present its source materials in a more marginal way, with the information presented more idiosyncratically, such as a bibliography that is in no discernible order.

4.3.7 Common pitfalls

As a student of sports history, it is easy to fall into a number of traps when using secondary sources for assignments.

The first trap is failing to reflect on the nature of your secondary sources. You may choose to use only one type of source without reflecting on that genre's nature, and its strengths and weaknesses. Journal articles, for example, are often easily accessible and quick to read, while using websites requires little activity. All sports historians should use all of the genres covered in this chapter, and should think through their nature and limitations. An assignment based only on articles, or popular histories, or websites, will inevitably be weak.

Secondly, many students start their reading thinking only about their assignment title, and then expecting all of the reading they do to fit into that title's terms of reference. You need to appreciate that the historiography exists independently of your essay, and that nothing will be written in a way that is tailored to your specific needs. Assuming that the answers are waiting to be harvested from a few books and websites is dangerous. You need to be more active and creative than this in your research, and to involve yourself in the debates.

Third, many students often fail to ask basic historiographical questions of the sources and their authors. At the very least, such a failure will lead to essays that are weak on interpretation and debate. More seriously, it can lead you into basic errors of fact, as in the failure to note which war is being referred to by the author, or the recognition that historians of rugby league, rugby union, association football, American football, Canadian football, and Australian rules football all use the word 'football' in their texts but mean six different sports.

Finally, many students feel that they have to read everything on a booklist or the library shelf, and feel disheartened when they realise that this is impossible due to time constraints. You need to develop good study skills to help you through this. For example, it is often useful to start with the more general items on a reading list, such as textbooks or works of synthesis, then work into the more specialised writings once you have got a sense of the key issues. Use indexes and contents pages to help you focus in on the most significant sections, and always read introductions and conclusions to monographs so that you can see what the main arguments and findings are. This is not necessarily the most enjoyable way to read history, but you can always return to the most interesting items in your own time.

▶ 4.4 Conclusion

This chapter has been designed to help you avoid such traps. The themes covered have been driven by my assumption that just as we cannot understand sport unless we look at it in the context of the time and the place in which it happened, so we cannot understand the historiography unless we ask the same questions of it. A sports history textbook has to be seen in the contexts of mass education, the publishing industry, and the historical research already carried out. A sports history website needs to be seen in the context of the political economy of the Internet, the popularisation of history in a postindustrial society, and the mass availability of personal computers. Look for these contexts, and work with them. By embracing historiography and thinking historiographically about everything you do, and by recognising the contexts, remits, limitations, and strengths of any source you use, you will become far more critical and effective than if you simply take texts at face value.

Activity 2: Audit

To help you get the maximum benefit from any text you use, it is worth running it through a historiographical audit. View this as analogous to a warm-up before a sporting activity. If you go in to a match cold, you run the risk of picking up an injury. If you try to read a historian's work cold, you run the risk of missing out on some of its basic features, ranging from the author's point of view and ideology through to the conventions of the genre. Try an audit approach to get into this habit. Once you are used to it, it will become second nature for you to run every text through this kind of check.

1. Identify the text you need (for example, from a reading list) and locate it.

2. Find out when and where it was published, and think about what was going on at that time that might have had a bearing on how historians viewed sport.

3. Find out what you can about the author: gender, ethnicity, age at the time of writing, nationality, religion, profession, teaching interests, and other publications.

4. Bring points 2 and 3 together and think how these factors might have affected the historian's approach to the subject matter.

5. Find out what you can about the text's intended audience by looking at its style and language, its publisher, its price, its treatment of sources, and its structure.

6. Look at the sources that the author has used so that you can gauge the depth and the breadth of the study.

7. Identify the genre that the book most obviously falls into, and use it accordingly.

5 Primary Evidence

► ## 5.1 The importance of primary evidence

Primary evidence is the foundation of all historical research. Unless we have evidence from the time that we are studying, we cannot conduct historical research. As a student, you will use primary evidence in various forms. You will access some through reproductions in textbooks, or through quotations in monographs and articles, and you are likely to use some selected by your tutor in class handouts. If you do a dissertation or special project in sports history, then you are likely to locate and use some primary evidence yourself, independent of the authors and tutors who have made the selections mentioned above. The higher the level at which you are working, the more primary evidence you will use, and the more independent judgement you will need to exercise in evaluating and analysing that evidence. This chapter is designed to help you develop a critical perspective on primary evidence as a whole, and to give you some insights on why and how you can use them. It is followed in Chapters 6 and 7 by a more detailed discussion of the main types of primary evidence that you, as a sports historian, are likely to come across.

In Chapter 1, we introduced the important point that without evidence, there can be no history. History is the study of the human past, and for any study to take place there has to be evidence. Imagine some scenarios from other areas of sports studies to put this in perspective. Unless you gather data in a laboratory or similar environment, you will not be able to conduct any sports physiology experiments. Without interviews, observations, or questionnaires, sports psychology would be impossible. Think of sports history in the same way: no evidence, no study. However, the comparison with other parts of sports studies breaks down at this point. The big distinction is that in these scientific disciplines, it is you as the investigator who generates the evidence. Unless you specifically ask a designated group of people to perform your experiment or answer your questions, that data will not exist.

This is also the case in social science and management approaches to sport, such as those based in sociology and business studies, where the researcher's completed questionnaires, observation records, and interview transcripts form the primary evidence base. In sports history, on the other hand, the evidence already exists, and would exist whether you were interested in it or not. The minute books of a football club will sit filed away in an archive regardless of your involvement, and a historical site such as the Coliseum will remain where it is, whether you do a project on ancient Roman sport or one on the history of baseball in your home town. So, whereas the sports scientist's research is driven predominantly by the generation of original data where none existed before, the sports historian's research is based on locating, contextualising, and analysing a diverse range of materials that already exist, and linking them to the relevant secondary historiography. You need to appreciate this point before you can work as a sports historian at anything other than a superficial level. You also need to recognise that your work will be far more effective if you think about the nature of the sources you are using than if you simply accept them as gospel, or if you reject them all as limited and biased. A more sensible and sophisticated approach than this – one that recognises all sources' limitations and also respects the fact that they come from the past that we are studying, and are our links with that past – will be far more useful than such narrow-mindedness.

Chapters 6 and 7 will take you through some of the main forms of evidence that you are likely to encounter in your studies, either second hand through course materials or first hand through your own research. Such secondhand access is essential, but you will be most effective as a sports historian if you also use primary sources yourself, without the mediation and choice of lecturers and authors. However, even if you choose not to take this opportunity, an appreciation of the nature of primary sources will help you to get more out of the secondary sources that you use. After all, all of the historiography you use is based on its authors' own research, and you will achieve a deeper understanding of that literature if you can think critically about its research base. Before we look at the different types of primary evidence used by sports historians, a theme also explored in detail by Douglas Booth,[1] this chapter will flesh out the introductory remarks about the nature of historical evidence, and will suggest some questions to have in mind when approaching primary sources, and some general analytical techniques.

We have already argued that without primary sources – that is, evidence that was created at the time you are studying – there can be no history. We would have nothing to go on. In Chapter 2, we looked at some of the myths that have developed in people's accounts of certain sports' histories, such as the nineteenth-century shinty historian's belief that his favourite sport had been played in the Garden of Eden, or the rugby union myth of William Webb Ellis. Our claim as academic historians that these stories are myths is based on our observation that no one has ever found any evidence for them, and that the evidence that does exist suggests alternative, less simplistic and more realistic, histories. Primary evidence, then, is central to all historical enquiries. We need primary evidence so that we know what happened in the past, and so that we can get an insight to what people thought was happening. Primary evidence not only takes us into the events of the past, but can also give us a sense of the feelings, perceptions, and ideas of the people who lived in the past, and how they interpreted and perceived events. We also need primary evidence to know what the past looked like, both through mediated representations (such as pictures, paintings, films, maps) and through the physical remains themselves, such as artefacts (tools, clothing, sports equipment), buildings, and structured landscapes.

These brief examples should already have alerted you to the fact that the evidence base is diverse: historical research is not just about working on written documents in archives. Historians use diverse primary materials, and an appreciation of this diversity can help to show up the complexity of historical research. Simply, we could split sources down into written, visual, physical, and oral, although this disguises as much as it reveals. A newspaper, for example, would typically be classed as written, but this would ignore the illustrations and advertisements that are so important for a historian wanting a real feel for the source. It is thus desirable to think more creatively and holistically when developing a taxonomy, as Arthur Marwick has done. His list from 2001 ranges from 'documents of record' and 'polemical sources' to 'archaeology...and history on the ground' and 'oral traditions', and it is worthwhile reading his annotated list to get a sense of the variety.[2] A conscientious historian needs to be able to locate, contextualise, analyse, and synthesise evidence that comes in such different forms, each with its own conventions and styles. Many of the sources are unique, residing individually in archives or museums. Some of them are physical, such as artefacts, buildings, or landscapes. There is nothing simple about a historical research project that attempts to explore and balance out such different types of material.

Activity 1: Primary sources about you

To get a sense of the range of sources that historians use, imagine that a historian wished to write your biography, covering your family background and your life from birth to the present. While he or she could begin by interviewing you, he or she would also need primary evidence — sources created at the different times in your life under consideration. Write a list of the items that exist for such a project, under the following headings:

1. Official documents (such as your birth certificate, school records, and tax records)

2. Visual evidence (such as photographs of you or pictures you have drawn)

3. Personal evidence (such as diaries and letters)

4. Published evidence (such as newspaper stories about you or items in a school magazine)

5. Interviewees (other people who the historian could interview to find out about your past)

You should aim to have at least five items under each heading.
Now ask the following questions of that evidence base:

1. What facts about you would this give the historian?

2. What would this evidence tell the historian about your feelings, beliefs, and perceptions at different times in your life?

3. What would the historian learn about what your past looked like from this evidence?

▶ 5.2 The selection of primary evidence

From this example, it should be clear that one of the historian's biggest tasks is the selection of primary sources. Although not all periods and subjects have as much evidence as each other, there is still a mass of material that historians can potentially use. The idea of a historian locating every source of information relevant to his or her research is an attractive one. However, as John Tosh reminds us, 'Historical sources encompass every kind of evidence that human beings have left of their past activities',[3] so it is never possible for any historian to see everything. This is due both to the sheer size of the possible evidence we could use for any project, as suggested by Tosh, and to the fact that many relevant sources that did once exist no longer survive. Fires, floods, wars, rats, carelessness, and deliberate destruction mean that large parts of the human past are no longer accessible. Because of this, we need to think about the role of selection in historical research. It is only if a historian chooses to research a minute part of sports history that he or she will manage to see everything – say, the history of a sports club in a year or two of its development, where all surviving club archives and local newspapers may be accessible. Seeing everything relevant is also possible if you decide to let the limits of your research project be defined by the surviving sources rather than by bigger themes. However, both of these approaches would create history that is both limited and limiting. It is more realistic to admit that it is impossible to see every relevant primary source, and to recognise the role that selection plays in historical research.

This can be illustrated by a personal recollection based on my first major sports history research, my PhD on the British Foreign Office and international sport in the first half of the twentieth century. My lengthy and detailed work in the Foreign Office archives at the Public Record Office (now the National Archives) meant that, over the course of my three years of full-time research, I should ideally have seen every relevant document. I did use hundreds of files containing thousands of individual papers, such as letters, memoranda, minutes of meetings, telegrams, and press cuttings. Some of them were small, such as one line telegrams; others were reports up to a hundred pages in length. Taken together, and making links to the existing scholarship of both sport and diplomacy, I was able to tell a fairly full story of what happened, and analyse many features of British sports diplomacy in this period.

However, when we revisit this process in the light of the problem of selection, a few problems come into view. First, I did not see any papers that did not survive. This is a truism, but one that cannot be understated. Comparing the original Foreign Office indexes with the list of papers in the archive, it is clear that many files have been destroyed. The reasons for this destruction rest more on the Foreign Office's view of sport as ephemeral and irrelevant than on any conspiracy, but the result is the same for historians: the evidence has gone. Second, I cannot guarantee that I saw all the papers that have survived, as some may have been poorly indexed, or indexed in a way that was useful for the original audience but useless for me as a historian. Historians involved in any form of primary research are heavily dependent on the work of earlier indexers and archivists. While we can often reconstruct once we have a few leads, we can never be sure that individual papers or files that we would index under, in this case, sport were not indexed under something else when they were first created. Third, while I did plenty of lateral research on individual cases of sports diplomacy, I may have missed material in the archives of other government departments with which the Foreign Office had to deal. For example, the 1935 football match between England and Germany generated action in, at least, the Foreign Office, the Home Office, the Metropolitan Police, and London Transport. Multiply this by all the other government departments and statutory agencies involved in sport, and the chances of missing material are increased. Fourth, I may have missed material through earlier officials' random acts or deliberate deceptions. A good example of this is a missing letter from a Foreign Office file about the 1908 Olympics. The files show that William Davidson, the Foreign Office's Legal Advisor, agreed to write a personal letter to Lord Desborough of the British Olympic Association about a French complaint. The minute setting that letter up survives in the Foreign Office file, but the letter itself does not, presumably as the author wanted to make it as unofficial as possible. Days of legwork and a trip to Buckinghamshire County Record Office located the letter in Desborough's private papers, an illustration of the logistical problems that face historians; in this minor case, two days' work on various indexes and reference books, plus a 150-mile-round trip from home to the record office, to find one letter, indicates how time-consuming historical research can be. These problems are being reduced by archive offices' increasing use of online catalogues and selective digitisation of records, but you will still usually have to visit the relevant collection to see the original. However, while I traced that letter I cannot know of all the similar papers that have been

dispersed from the central archive. Finally, my project was limited –
by title and resources – to concentrate on the actions of the Foreign
Office and its related bodies, and I did no more than scratch the surface
of many other relevant types of primary source, such as newspapers,
overseas governments' archives, personal papers, and the archives of
sports clubs and governing bodies. My PhD was detailed and thorough,
and it worked as a project: but it would be disingenuous of me, once
we consider the reflections above, to claim that I used every relevant
primary source. Every other honest historian would be able to give a
similar deconstruction of their work: in practice, selection of primary
sources happens, and we cannot pretend that we use everything that
was produced at the time we are studying, or even a tiny proportion of
everything.

This personal illustration is designed to help you recognise the importance of selection when you are working in sports history, both as a
reader of other people's work and as a researcher on your own projects.
You can put it in context by comparing it to sports science research. No
physiology experiment can hope to cover all of the people in a target
population, so the researcher creates a representative sample from
which, it is hoped, results can be extrapolated onto wider groups, and
valid conclusions can be drawn that can be applied across the board.
A sports psychology project will similarly use a case study or sampling
approach. So the idea of selection within sports studies is not unique
to the discipline of history. However, you need to think critically about
the specific circumstances of selection in historical research, and to
recognise the types of selection that go on around historical evidence.
If you consider this, then you will be able to recognise how selection
shapes both what you see in your own primary research and what you
see as the basis of existing historiography. Think about it at two levels.
First, there is the issue of survival from the past, and the processes of
selection that go on to allow some materials to come to us while others
are lost. This is the type of selection that whittles down the vast bank of
all the possible primary sources into the much smaller bank of evidence
that we keep. Different criteria and patterns have affected the selection of the different types of evidence that sports historians use. For
example, physical spaces such as stadiums tend to survive for as long
as they are useful, whereas documentary evidence – by its nature more
ephemeral, more fragmentary, and more perishable – needs to have
specific protection in order to survive. Second, there is the process by
which historians make further selections from the surviving materials
on which to base their work, as exemplified by my case study above. As
with secondary sources, there is an element of 'horses for courses' here:

historians will use the sources that will help them answer their research questions. E.H. Carr, in *What is History?*, made a fishing analogy that can help us focus on this relationship:

> The facts [of history] . . . are like fish swimming about in a vast and some-times inaccessible ocean; and what the historian catches will depend, partly on chance, but mainly on what part of the ocean he chooses to fish in and what tackle he chooses to use – these two factors being, of course, determined by the kind of fish he wants to catch.[4]

In applied terms, this is simply about recognising that different kinds of primary evidence will tell you different things about the period under analysis. A photograph can tell you what a sporting event looked like, a minute book can tell you how it was organised, an accounts book can tell you how much money it made or lost, a newspaper can tell you who won, and a player's autobiography can tell you what it felt like to play. This comes back to selection: you cannot see every piece of evidence, so you have to choose which pieces to use; and your choice will be influenced by the kind of inform-ation you want. This element of choice helps us to remember the role of the historian's theoretical perspective: someone working in a Marxist tradition, for example, is likely to choose types of evid-ence that will reveal something about class. It also underlines the role of individual interpretation in history writing: different histor-ians with different questions and concerns can interpret the same materials in different ways. Recognising the relationship between what the sports historian wants to know and the evidence that he or she uses is an important step towards a critical appreciation of historical research. Each one is valid within its own terms, and the selection of sources is justified by the nature of the project. As you develop your secondary reading skills, you will recognise the kind of selections that have gone on in the historiography, and so learn by example what the most promising kinds of sources for your own original research could be.

Activity 2: Identifying other historians' primary evidence

All academic sports historians provide a record of the primary evidence on which their published research is based. This record appears in each text's references. Select three journal articles by any three academic sports historians, and find their references: these may appear in a reference list at the end of the text, or as a series of endnotes, depending on the journal's house style. Read through the references, and compile a list of every type of source that is used (for example, 'newspaper', 'club minutes'). This basic activity will give you an idea of the range of sources that are available for sports history, and it may show the more popular types of evidence. Once you have completed this task, make sure that you always check for the evidence base of every sports history text that you use.

▶ 5.3 Dealing with primary sources

In real historical research, the selection and analysis of primary evidence are not as clear-cut as they may sound at first. Historians will constantly find new material and choose not to use sources that they had found earlier, and it is only through careful and comparative analysis, always linked back to the project's aims, that the final selection of evidence is made. Historians have to be prepared for serendipitous discoveries, similar to those discussed in Chapter 4 on secondary sources. Although they will have an idea of the kind of information they want from any given primary source, they cannot know what it really contains until they study it, and so they need to be prepared to accommodate new themes as they arise out of the evidence. This may mean refocusing a whole project, or it may mean identifying another area as a topic for further research. Either way, the ability to be flexible is part of the open-mindedness that rigorous and conscientious historians bring to their work. However, for the purposes of this chapter, it is straightforward to separate selection from analysis. So, how do historians deal with the evidence that they find? What can you do with primary evidence to make your own research more academic? Again, Marwick has provided a most useful guide, which he calls a 'catechism for the analysis, evaluation and use of primary sources',[5] and you should read this for a detailed picture. For our purposes, we can simplify this approach by concentrating on four stages.

The first stage is about your intellectual approach to the act of primary research. You need to use a sense of critical respect, and this involves getting yourself into a state of mind that combines empathy and historical imagination with a hard line in awkward questioning. Once you are sure that a piece of evidence is genuine, and that it is from the time you are studying, you have to accept that it was there in the past and you were not. This idea should promote the sense of critical respect: respect because it can tell you something about a period that may otherwise be inaccessible to you; critical because you must not be overawed by its primacy into accepting it as gospel. You need to remember that every source you use (with very few exceptions) would have existed without your intervention. Even the exceptions, such as interviews that you conduct or field-based photographs that you take, are based on things that would exist without you – in these examples, people's memories and the physical landscape respectively – and which you are simply capturing in a new medium. You also need to appreciate that every source was created for purposes that were relevant at the time of its creation, and not for the benefit of historians such as you and me. We may be able to use them to deepen our understanding of the past, but they were not made for us. Once you are able to recognise these issues, and appreciate that you were not any source's intended audience, you will recognise the importance of placing all sources in their context, and you will be well placed to use them critically for your study.

Stage two, then, is about placing the source in its original context. This covers the general time and place at which it was created, and the specifics of its creation. You can find this out by asking the following questions of your source: Who created it? When was it created? Where was it created? Was its creator working on his or her own, or was he or she part of an organisation? Who was the source's original intended audience or user? Why was the source created? Without this spadework, which will often involve secondary reading around a piece of evidence, you may end up overlooking some crucial aspect of the source, or making anachronistic judgements about it.

Third, you need to analyse the source's content. What does it contain? In the case of a written document, this involves detailed reading to see both what it can tell us about the events in which we are interested and to see how it tells us this. For example, two newspaper accounts of the same cricket match could tell us the same basic information of scores, fall of wickets, and performances. However, each one will have been created for a different audience, and will have come out of a different context, so their style, language, and tone will differ: they will give us the same information in different ways. In the case of a non-written source, such as a picture, a film, an artefact, or a landscape, you still need to think about content: what does the source actually tell us about the time in which it was created. In all cases, the emphasis remains on the time of creation: what does it tell us about its creators and its audiences?

These two stages have required you to take the source as it was at its time of creation. The final stage is about getting further beneath the source's skin, and making it work for your project. This is the stage of source assessment. How useful, reliable, and valid is this piece of evidence? Why has it survived? What does its survival tell us about its significance? What does it tell us when placed along other sources from the same time? Does it confirm or challenge other evidence that we have? What particular skills do we need to use it? What have other historians made of it? This is what Marwick refers to as relating what a source tells us to 'knowledge obtained from other sources',[6] and it means that we have to be prepared to work out from the sources as often as possible. No primary source contains everything you need to know, and no source can be used in complete isolation, so you must be prepared to read around them to help make sense of them. This applies to such diverse aspects of sources as the exact contemporary meanings of words, the identity of people and places mentioned in newspapers, the artistic influences evident in a painting, and the contemporary technical specifications of cameras used to take specific pictures. Questioning its survival and maintenance can also lead you into considering the political nature of all archives, and you should reflect on Booth's analysis of the ways in which all organisations – especially governments and governing bodies – 'operate within a climate of confidentiality' in which they 'manipulate, conceal, hide and destroy information'.[7] Approach your primaries with a willingness to understand them, a willingness that requires you to read around.

The last three stages will help you set up the effective analysis of any primary evidence that you use. It is not easy, and it needs practice, particularly if you are researching across a range of source types. For example, a project on the history of a local golf club, which was based on minute books, newspapers, interviews with old members, maps and photographs of the course over the years, and contemporary field walking, would involve the researcher in impressive feats of mental gymnastics, as each source would require a different form of analysis. However, developing an organised way of managing each source, as in these stages of Marwick's catechism, can help you focus on each source individually, derive as much from each source as possible, and build up a comparative and holistic picture.

Finally, we need to cover some basic study skills that you must use when dealing with primary evidence. Whatever sources you are using, from private letters to statues, from government reports to novels, some ground rules apply.

Accurate transcription If you are transcribing any words, you must get them right. If you import mistakes, even minor spelling or grammatical ones, then you could end up misunderstanding the source and misrepresenting it in your own work. This rule applies to people's names, dates, and any other factual information that you are transcribing, too. If you spot an error in the original, then copy the error, but add the note *sic* (Latin for 'thus') in square brackets immediately after the mistake. This will show that the error was the original author's, and not yours.

Reliable copies of visual material If you are using visual evidence, such as photographs and paintings, you must devise a way of keeping good, reliable copies of them for analysis. This will not always be possible: if your source is a painting in a gallery, you will not be able to take it home. Look instead at such options as digital photography or a postcard of the painting. You will lose something in the translation, particularly size and true colours, but you will be able to study it in your own working environment. If you take your own photographs for your research, make sure that you date them.

Record-keeping Make sure that all notes that you make are accurately and fully titled, giving as much information as possible. This must include details of authors, titles, and, in the case of archival materials, the location of the records (which record office they are in) and the record office's unique registration number for the record. This information will help you reference the sources that you quote from or cite in your work, and it will give you a sense of control over the evidence that you collate. It will also allow you to engage with the published historiography: once you have used the same sources as those used by the historians whose work you are reading, you can get an enhanced insight to their work.

▶ 5.4 Conclusion

The themes covered in this chapter and the activities that you have done should have given you an idea of the role of primary evidence in sports history. Remember that without evidence there can be no history: we must have something from the past to go on. The evidence we use is varied, with different types of evidence telling us about different aspects of the past. In each case, though, we need to assess and analyse the evidence so that we understand it in its primary context. Without that step, it is easy to misuse the evidence in a number of ways. The easiest way for this to happen is through clumsiness, such as the mistranscription of a word from a document that we then repeat in a quotation. We can be anachronistic, for example, and take a piece of evidence out of its original context; and we can over-emphasise, and give a piece of evidence a significance that it did not have when it was created. Contextualising your evidence also helps you to avoid limiting your analysis by getting stuck in the search for bias. Remember that all primary evidence was created by people in the past for contemporary reasons, so it will always have ideologies and agendas from the time and the place of production built into it. This point should also help us see beyond the comfortable belief that some pieces of evidence will be objective and thus more valid. We may conventionally feel that some types of evidence are more reliable than others: for example, many students would feel more comfortable with a sports club's minute books than with a poem about sport. However, it is important to remember that both the minute book and the poem were created for particular reasons, in particular formats, and at particular times: each one is as much a historical source as the other, as they both come from the time that you, the historian, are studying. You will ask different questions of them, and consult them for insight to different aspects of the past. There is no point going to the poem if you want to know when a rule was changed, or in going to the minute book if you want to know how the sport was perceived in aesthetic terms at the time. Scholarly analysis carried out in an open-minded way, with an ear for nuance, can help you recognise and use subjectivity, and to build a multilayered impression of the past from different pieces of evidence.

Over the next two chapters, we move on to explore some of the types of primary evidence that sports historians use. These chapters will build on the general points covered in this chapter by critically introducing you to the kind of sources that you will find as the research base for the published work you read, and by encouraging you to look for primary sources for your own research. They are designed to help you make some sense of the variety and range of sources, and to encourage you to reflect on the nature, value, and limitations of different sources. Through this kind of consideration of each source's nature and identity, you can have realistic expectations of all the evidence you go to, and you can frame common types of questions according to each source's nature. Research widely and critically around the different types of source, and you can build up a detailed picture of the aspect of the past that you are studying.

In Chapters 6 and 7, then, we will consider different kinds of evidence. I have based the categorisation in part on Marwick's insightful taxonomy, and in part on the specifics of what sports historians use. In Chapter 6, we will explore sources of news and information, and sources of record and policy, and sources based on persuasion; then, in Chapter 7, we will look at artistic and creative sources, artefacts and archaeology, and sources based on memory. These thematic headings have been chosen as they will help you to focus on the nature of each type of evidence at its time of creation.

6 Primary Sources in Sports History 1

The themes and issues covered in Chapter 5 will have alerted you to the variety of primary sources that are available for historical research. In this chapter and Chapter 7, we are moving on from discussions about the nature of primary evidence, and the kind of steps you need to take when using them, to consider the different kinds of primary evidence that sports historians use. As you will have seen from Activity 2 in the previous chapter, historians use many different types of evidence, ranging from minute books to newspapers, from films to artefacts, and from interviews to novels. Each different type has its own particular strengths and weaknesses, and each one requires particular skills. Moreover, you need to be realistic in your expectations of what kind of sources exist, and what kind of information you can get from different types of source, and you must ensure that the sources you use are relevant to the nature of your project.

To help you identify what kinds of sources may be relevant, and to help you structure your expectations about the evidence, let us now look in overview at the types of sources available. Obviously, the quantity of different sources available varies hugely from time to time and place to place, both in terms of what was produced and what has survived to the present. You therefore need to do some wider research into the period you are studying, before you look for specific sources for sports history: there is no point, for example, in looking for photographic evidence if you are studying a period before the invention of the camera. If you couple this kind of informed approach with a sense of realism about what your sources can and cannot be expected to tell you, then you should be able to work professionally and responsibly with the primary evidence.

In this chapter, we will look at newspapers and magazines, film and broadcast media, government records, club and governing body records, other organisations' records, and private papers. These will be followed in Chapter 7 by advertisements, polemical sources, creative literature, fine art and photography, feature films, ephemera and artefacts, landscapes and maps, memoirs, and interviews. You should use these chapters in conjunction with Richard Cox's invaluable *History of Sport: A Guide to the Literature and Sources of Information* and the British Society of Sports History's online Sports History Archives/Manuscripts listing as guides to more detailed resources on some of the themes covered here.[1] Some of the types of evidence discussed in these chapters have exercises attached so that you can practise primary source analysis. Most of these take the form of fairly long extracts from primary sources. Rather than set leading questions on these, which could be repetitive and limiting, you should approach each one in the way suggested in the four-stage audit explained in Chapter 5: apply your sense of critical respect, then analyse its context and content, before assessing its significance as a source. In each case, for example, you need to find out what you can about the author, and about what was going on at the time the piece was created; and you always need to analyse the content, both for what it tells us and for how it tells it. To give you some leads, I have, instead of questions, suggested some themes that are worth considering. In addition, the Bibliography contains a section on Web-based resources that will help you locate primary sources on many aspects of sports history.

▶ 6.1 Newspapers and magazines

Newspapers, magazines, and their forerunners the broadsheets, have long been valued by sports historians. Through them, we can get both information about sport in the past – the events, the results, the players, the geographical distribution of sport, and so on – and a sense of what sport meant to the people involved in it. Newspapers and magazines have always created sports stars, and the way in which they have been reported tells us a lot about the wider tastes and mores of the time. As well as sports news coverage, newspapers and magazines can also be used for pictures, originally posed shots, but with improvements in camera technology from the 1920s, of sporting action, too. Sports historians can also gain from going beyond the sports pages and looking at other sections. Sporting events have often been covered as news, particularly in times of crisis: the 1972 Olympic crisis, for example, dominated front pages around the world. Newspapers driven by sensation and gossip have long held a fascination with the private lives of famous sportsmen and women, and this is likely to be contained in society or gossip pages. Editorial columns and letters pages are also key resources, as they take us into comments, debates, and controversies about sport. Finally, advertisements in sports sections for sports good and services tell us something about the products themselves, and about the assumed audiences of each newspaper or magazine, and their disposable income. However, despite the obvious appeal that newspapers and magazines have for sports historians because of their widespread coverage, a number of commentators have criticised sports historians' indiscriminate over-reliance on the press. This argument has been recently crystallised by Jeff Hill. He stresses the ways in which the 'narrative structures'[2] used by journalists and editors inevitably place a distance between events themselves and the news stories of those events; but that, at the same time, the press has been the main way in which people in the past have experienced real sport. Newspapers, then, should not be seen simply as easy repositories of facts about sport – fixture lists, results, reports, and so on – but as sources of stories about sport: as Hill puts it, 'anecdotal evidence'.

Newspapers and magazines are widely accessible to researchers, through local library collections, media company archives, and national collections such as the British Library Newspaper Library. Such holdings can never be complete, especially for a product as ephemeral and physically fragile as a daily newspaper: but they are comprehensive, particularly as microfilming and digitisation have allowed originals to be protected. If you are considering using newspapers, you should look widely, and not just stick at obvious titles such as *The Times* for the UK or *The Washington Post* for the USA. Local and regional newspapers, and specialised sports papers and magazines, can provide far more detail and variety. Indeed, you can discover a great deal about debates on sport in the period under research by reading comparatively. For example, the political crisis caused by the England v Germany football match of 1935 can be seen from many perspectives if it is researched through an establishment newspaper like *The Times*, the German Government's official *Völkische Beobachter*, conservative titles such as *The Daily Mail*, the Communist Party's *Daily Worker*, a newspaper local to the match's location, *The Tottenham and Edmonton Weekly Herald*, and a football magazine such as *Football Pictorial*. All of these newspapers covered the controversial build up to the match, taking different angles on its sporting and political significance. When using newspapers and magazines, you need to read around each title's politics, market, and ownership, and consider these as contextual to any sports coverage. Think, for example, of media cross-ownership that might make a newspaper write only positive stories about a sport that is carried exclusively on a related television channel; or of the attitude towards women's sport that you are likely to find in a newspaper that includes photographs of topless women on its other pages. It is also important to consider the time lag between events and the newspaper appearing. In many cases, the short-time lags that newspapers have established are helpful, as they give us first-hand accounts written within hours of the event. However, the need to meet deadlines can also create mistakes, particularly, in a sporting context, in the coverage of crowd disasters such as those at Ibrox in 1902 or Hillsborough in 1989. Here, over- or under-estimations of casualties, and premature speculation about causes, can make newspapers unreliable for facts, in line with Hill's criticisms, but still useful for perceptions.

Activity 1: Extracts from a report in *The Times* (London) of 30 September 1811 on the prize fight between Tom Crib, the English champion, and Tom Molyneux, an American former slave

The battle betwixt the formidable champion *Crib* and the powerful *Molineaux* which has been the first and only consideration amongst the sporting world, took place on Saturday at Thissleton Gap in the county of Rutland. A 25 feet stage was erected in a stubble-ground, and before 12 o'clock several thousands of persons had collected, the one-fourth of whom were Nobility and Gentry from the surrounding country. Not a bed could be had within 20 miles of the seat of action of Friday night...

Round 1. Sparring for one minute, when Crib made play, right and left. A rally followed in which three blows were exchanged, when the Black was knocked down by a blow on the throat. The knock-down was not clean.

. . .

Round 3. Crib's right eye was nearly closed. After sparring for wind, in which the Black was deficient, Crib put in a dreadful doubler to the body of the Moor, but although he was hit away, he kept his legs and renewed the rally with a fury which excited alarm amongst the Cognoscenti. Crib in the rally hit left and right at the body and head, and the Moor fought at the head alone, and was so successful with the left hand that he planted some dexterous flush hits, and Crib bled profusely and was damaged in both eyes.

4. Crib's head was much disfigured, and the Black's wind was treacherous. The former bled from every organ, but he smiled, renewed the rally with heroism never excelled, and hits in abundance were exchanged.

...

6. Crib put in a destructive right-handed blow at the Black's body, which doubled him up who got away pitifully distressed. He appeared frantic on renewing a rally, and no dancing-master ever cut capers more amusing to Crib's friends. He hit short and was abroad. Crib followed him around the stage and did astonishing execution and floored him with a blow at great length.

7. Molineaux ran in on a rally intemperately and did some execution, but Crib hit him several blows as violent as can be figured about the neck and jugular, and the Moor fell from hurts and weakness.

8. Molineaux in the forlorn hope again rallied at ill-judged distance, and after Crib had again nobbed him, he got his head under the left arm, and fibbed until the Moor fell.

The battle may be here considered as terminated. In the next round Crib broke his antagonists' jaw, and at the close of the 11th round, Molineaux being unable to stand, victory was announced in a Scot's reel by Gully [Crib's second] and Crib.

Themes to explore:

1. The language and quality of the reporting style, and the assumed levels of education and sporting knowledge amongst the newspaper's readers.

2. The level of detail in the report.

3. The degree of violence involved in prize fighting at this time.

▶ 6.2 Film and broadcast news media

By the end of the nineteenth century, moving image technology was being applied to sporting events. Since then, newsreel and wireless coverage of sport from the 1920s, and then television coverage, means that there is a vast archive of film and sound news-based materials on sport. As we get closer to the present, this includes entire events – whole matches, full marathons, and so on – as well as highlights. Through these media, we can literally see the events happening and, in many cases, hear the real noises of the crowd, while also hearing how contemporary commentators reported on sport. Such sources are invaluable to sports historians. They can give us a realistic image of so many features of the sport: what the players looked like, how they moved, their tactics and strategies, crowd sizes and behaviour, stadium design, and so much more. This type of source is simply peerless for sports historians. However, they also have their limitations: remember that every aspect of a film or broadcast is highly selective, and we as historians can see only what the makers and editors of the piece chose to include. This is particularly true in selective newsreels, where the 90 minutes of an FA Cup final were reduced into under 2 minutes of footage, but it is also the case in any other broadcast or film.

To use this type of source effectively, you will need to know something about the technology that was used to create it. Of what were the cameras and microphones capable? How was footage edited? What were the limitations of the film or sound media used for the recording? What did it cost to make? You will also need to consider intended audiences, as this will have shaped the original product. A 1930s cinema newsreel, or the *March of Time* films in the USA, for example, was designed to be shown as part of an evening's entertainment for millions of people in a public place, and sport was only a small part of its remit; whereas the BBC's broadcast version of the 2003 Rugby Union World Cup Final was designed for home and pub consumption as a significant live event. In each case, particular devices and codes were used to suit the audience and media type, and you will need to analyse these in order to understand and interpret the sporting action that you see. Access to such evidence has become easier since the inception of the Internet, as many holdings are now available online: Pathe, for example, has thousands of clips that are searchable and free for download for educational purposes, and the BBC is making selections of archive news clips available for free viewing, including some on sporting themes.[3] While these are usually only small samples, they can give you something to work on and act as an introduction to the source. Fuller versions are available in various locations. Local record offices often hold film and sound archives relevant to their region. National collections, such as the British Library's National Sound Archive and the British Film Institute, all hold relevant primary materials, while transcripts and supporting materials can be researched in such holdings as the BBC's Written Archive Centre.

▶ 6.3 Government records

Governments of all types and ideologies have always had an interest in sport, and the records that they have created are a valuable resource for sports historians. The range of issues and events covered in such records is enormous, and the quantity of evidence varies from place to place and time to time: Communist governments, for example, have historically taken a far greater role in the planning and management of sport than governments operating in liberal democratic traditions; while evidence for the modern period has been more likely to survive than anything from medieval and ancient times. However, what is available tells us much about sport itself, and about its interrelationship with the state. There are many themes that we can identify in government records on sport. Governments have, through law-making, created the statutory environment in which sports take place, and the evidence of these laws – both the statutes themselves and, where available, the parliamentary and departmental debates that led up to the legislation – is rich for sports historians. It tells us about why some sporting activities have been banned or permitted at certain times. This evidence also tells us how events that were permitted have been constrained or structured by legislation, ranging from bars on interracial sport in Nazi Germany and apartheid South Africa through to health and safety requirements in contemporary capitalist societies in which insurance and litigation concerns are high. Governments have historically taken on the role of provider of sport, through such channels as state schools, local authority sports facilities, and promotion bodies such as the Sports Council, and these have left records that can tell us about governors' assumptions, social problems such as disorder, poverty, and public health, and the growth of state responsibility. Sports diplomacy has been a major feature of sport since the early twentieth century, with governments and sport interacting to make statements about other countries. The Olympic boycotts of 1976, 1980, and 1984, for example, were statements of disapproval and condemnation, while the British government's decision to promote sporting links with Germany during the 1930s was a statement about normality and appeasement. In all cases, the archives of diplomatic correspondence take us into the ideas, ideologies, compromises, and decision-making involved in this aspect of sports history. Another type of evidence to consider here is that of state involvement in major sporting events, such as Olympic Games and the football World Cup, where investment in infrastructure and tourism around the sport can tell us about the events themselves, and about how sport has fitted into wider policies of regeneration and investment. Finally, we should consider demographic evidence created by governments, such as census and taxation records. These can provide us with contextual information about populations, occupational trends, and services, and with detailed personal information on individuals who were involved in sport in the period under analysis.

Central and local government records, in these and other areas, are a rewarding resource for sports historians. In all of these areas, the quantity of surviving and accessible primary evidence varies greatly depending on the period and country that you are researching. The more recent your period, the more there will be. This is mainly because the growth of state interest in sport has been a relatively recent phenomenon (certainly when compared to central government records on taxation, religion, and military affairs, for example). It is also caused by the growing realisation in the archiving industry that sport matters, so more material is being preserved properly. Some of the types of evidence covered here are available in published formats, such as the texts of all laws, the published reports of government committees, and the results of censuses. Much of the material is available only in state-run record offices, such as the National Archives (formerly the Public Record Office) in the UK and the National Archives in the USA. This is usually the case when the material is unique (such as hand-written memoranda and background correspondence), and when a full record is needed. Historians' access to these archives is variable. In some places, sources are not opened until a set period of time after their creation, such as the 30 years in the UK's case. This presents a major limitation for the sports historian: for example, under the 30-year rule, no historian can research the British government's papers on the boycott of the 1980 Moscow Olympic Games until 2011. In others countries, material is available far quicker, while some governments maintain close control over their archives, and allow access only to approved researchers. The Internet is improving access, most obviously to catalogues and indexes, and also in some cases to whole documents. To make the most of these sources, you need to use a variety of skills. We can use skills based on textual and contextual analysis to work out what happened and why, and can gain insights to the links between sport and different political ideologies in history. Some of the evidence can also be analysed numerically, notably the census-type materials, allowing the sports historian to build up profiles of what sport was like at given times. However, to make the most of this material you need to be flexible, as you will often need to jump between different types of evidence in order to get all of the significant documents in a case study. You must remember that the evidence was created and compiled for contemporary reasons of governance, and not for your convenience. Moreover, you need to read widely on the political history of the period in order to make the most of this material. For example, if you research the primary evidence on the USA's boycott of the 1980 Moscow Olympic Games without having read around in the political and military history of US–Soviet relations at that time, then you are likely to miss nuances and connections that the authors of the documents took for granted.

Activity 2: The commonwealth statement on apartheid in sport, Gleneagles Hotel, 14 June 1977[4]

The member countries of the Commonwealth, embracing peoples of diverse races, colours, languages and faiths, have long recognized racial prejudice and discrimination as a dangerous sickness and an unmitigated evil and are pledged to use all their efforts to foster human dignity everywhere. . .

They were conscious that sport is an important means of developing and fostering understanding between the people, and especially between the young people, of all countries. But, they were also aware that, quite apart from other factors, sporting contacts between their nationals and the nationals of countries practising apartheid in sport tend to encourage the belief (however unwarranted) that they are prepared to condone this abhorrent policy or are less than totally committed to the principles embodied in their Singapore declaration. Regretting past misunderstandings and difficulties and recognizing that these were partly the result of inadequate inter-governmental consultations, they agreed that they would seek to remedy this situation in the context of the increased level of understanding now achieved.

They reaffirmed their full support for the international campaign against apartheid and welcomed the efforts of the United Nations to reach universally accepted approaches to the question of sporting contact within the framework of that campaign.

Mindful of these and other considerations, they accepted it as the urgent duty of each of their Governments vigorously to combat the evil of apartheid by withholding any form of support for, and by taking every practical step to discourage, contact or competition by their nationals with sporting organizations, teams or sportsmen from South Africa or from any other country where sports are organized on the basis of race, colour or ethnic origin.

They fully acknowledged that it was for each Government to determine in accordance with its laws the methods by which it might best discharge these commitments. But they recognized that the effective fulfilment of their commitments was essential to the harmonious development of Commonwealth sport hereafter.

They acknowledged also that the full realization of their objectives involved the understanding, support and active participation of the nationals of their countries and of their national sporting organizations and authorities. As they drew a curtain across the past they issued a collective call for that understanding, support and participation with a view to ensuring that in this matter the peoples and Governments of the Commonwealth might help to give a lead to the world.

Themes to explore:

1. The relationship between political ideology and sporting ideology embodied in this document.

2. The relationship between the Commonwealth as a unit and the countries that comprised it.

3. The balance between the polemical language of the statement and the nature of the commitments embodied in it.

▶ 6.4 Club and governing body records

Sports clubs have been formed for many different reasons and out of many different settings, including workplaces, places of worship, pubs, schools, and neighbourhoods; and while some went on to become leading bodies in their sports, such as the Marylebone Cricket Club (MCC, founded 1787) and the Jockey Club (founded 1750), the majority have been, and remain, the organisational focus for the playing of sport. Records of clubs' foundations, which can survive in minute books, correspondence, and press coverage, provide historians with some basic factual information, such as the names of those involved and the location of their meetings. More critical and contextual reading allows us to get a sense of each club's ethos and social status. For example, the level of formality used in minutes and correspondence, the titles (Mr, Mrs, Dr, Sir, Lady, Captain, and so on) of the members, and the value of subscriptions can all be read in the light of the period's social and economic history so that we can see what kind of people were involved in the club. These same sources can also take us into the club's day-to-day and season-to-season operation. From such records we can learn details of matches, players, and competitions, alongside details of by-laws, regulations, and rules. This material can allow you to develop links beyond one club and into others with whom they played, with evidence from different clubs accumulating to give a sense of the bigger picture of what that sport was like. This evidence can also show up links between the club and any central governing body, which may have been negotiated in correspondence, disciplinary procedures, and law changes during the period you are studying. Club records can also provide evidence of changes within a club itself, which you can relate to the wider context. For example, rises or falls in membership fees can tell us about the club's changing demographic profile over time, while evidence of a club's land use and ownership helps us to build up sense of its relative wealth, its presence in, and economic contribution to, its community, and its national importance. Clubs' constitutions and standing orders show us their legal and commercial status. Analysis of committee minutes over time allows us to track individuals, particularly interesting if you want to see the role played by players after their retirement. It also allows us to see the changing remit of a club over time, such as the development of youth teams, the inclusion or exclusion of women, and the relationship with commercial sponsors and the media. Any clubs that were instituted as businesses will also have left business records behind, such as those used by Wray Vamplew in his *Pay Up and Play the Game.*[5] Overall, club records are amongst the most basic primary materials of sports history, as they take us into the reasons for sport happening as it did, and the events of history.

Governing bodies – at national and, later, international (or supra-national) level – historically emerged after clubs. In some cases, such as those of the Jockey Club and the MCC cited above, leading clubs evolved into what amounted to governing bodies for a period; in others, interested parties from various clubs joined together to form governing bodies, usually as an association, a union, or a federation. Just as the clubs were formed to protect the interests of people who wanted to play sport together, so governing bodies emerged to ensure that those interests were protected, and the sport maintained and organised, at a higher level. As with the clubs, evidence of foundation will vary, but will typically reside in minute books, correspondence, records of meetings, and newspaper coverage. This material is a way into the personalities, the power groups, and the politics that are involved in the formation of any body. It is particularly useful for the early days of any governing body. In line with the theme of invented traditions explored in Chapter 2, governing bodies typically present their own birth in straightforward terms: detailed analysis of the records of origin tells us how complicated these matters really were, particularly when different groups laid claim to names and ideas. Adrian Harvey's detailed analysis of the power struggles between football groups based in Sheffield and London during the 1860s and 1870s is an excellent example of how governing bodies' records can provide us with detailed accounts of a sport's history.[6] At the international level, the archives of Fédération Internationale de Football Association (FIFA) have been fruitfully mined by historians to show the ways in which different national bodies, each with their own interests and concerns, came together to create an overall world organisation for the sport.[7]

Such records are also invaluable for evidence of the day-to-day running of any sport for which they survive. While this material may seem, on the face of it, to be dry in comparison to press coverage and players' memoirs, there is no substitute for getting into the archives of a sports organisation to see that sport's development and evolution. For example, the committee papers of the Amateur Athletics Association (AAA) are essential reading for anyone wishing to understand the battle between professionalism and amateurism in British athletics in the 1960s and 1970s, as they chart the decisions about advertising and sponsorship, the changing committee structures to match the changing times, and the disciplinary records of athletes punished for breaking the strict amateur rule.[8] Through such archives, we can find the administrative history of our sport.

However, this genre of evidence has not survived well. Tony Mason, in his *Association Football and English Society 1863–1915* of 1980, put the case bluntly:

> The vast majority of football clubs of the period 1863–1915 have disappeared without trace and particularly without leaving behind them such things as written records.[9]

This problem is not restricted to football. Clubs, particularly but not exclusively small ones, tended not to preserve records. The reasons for this include lack of time, lack of expertise, or the simple problem of records getting lost in the handover from one honorary post holder to the next. Things have improved since 1980, when Mason complained that no professional clubs had archivists and few professional archivists were interested in football: as we have seen in Chapter 3, the archive industry is now attuned to sport, and there are many special collections in professional hands, such as the AAA archive in the University of Birmingham's Special Collections Office and the Cyclists Touring Club's papers in Warwick University's Modern Records Centre. However, archivists cannot recreate what has been lost or destroyed. This means that the clubs we have records for are in a minority, so many of our conclusions – about any sport's social profile, or its costs – are based on what may be atypical case studies. A second problem faced by researchers is that clubs and governing bodies can refuse or restrict access to their archives. Clubs and governing bodies often remain sceptical of researchers' motivations and intentions, and can easily prevent anyone in who may be concerned with potentially sensitive issues, such as politics and financial management. This problem is being ameliorated by the transfer of club and governing body records to professional archives, as exemplified above, and by the growing trend of bodies appointing academic historians to write their official histories, such as the Welsh Rugby Union, the International Council of Sport Science and Physical Education, and FIFA.[10]

These issues of survival and access cannot be ignored: they have a major influence on the historical research that can be done. However, there is still plenty of evidence available, and it needs a variety of skills. Broadly, these are the same as those needed for government archives: textual analysis; contextual reading around to make sense of the references; a good understanding of the paper flow and decision-making process within the organisation; and a willingness to look for external materials – newspapers, memoirs, other organisations' records – to fill the gaps you may find. You also need to remember that despite the official and authorised status of such records, they are no more neutral or objective than any other kind of evidence. An organisation's minutes and reports are created within that organisation, and for its purposes, and they will embody its traditions, concerns, ideologies, and internal politics. For example, minutes tend to record decisions rather than reflect debates, and if we take them only at face value as the official version of what happened, then we will be closing our ears to the nuances that may exist to suggest dissent and alternatives.

Activity 3: Minutes of a Meeting of the International Football Association Board, April 1913[11]

Minutes of Meeting Held at 42, Russell Square, London, Friday 4th April, 1913.

Present Mr T.E. Thomas (Football Association of Wales), in the chair, Messrs. J.R. Stephens (Football Association of Wales), C. Crump and W. Pickford (Football Association), A.M. Robertson and D. Campbell (Scottish Football Association), H. Megan and J. MacBride (Irish Football Association).

There were also in attendance Messrs. T. Steen (Scottish Football Association), F.J. Wall (Secretary, Football Association), J. M'Dowall (Secretary, Scottish Football Association), J. Ferguson (Irish Football Association), and T. Robbins (Secretary, Football Association of Wales), who acted as Secretary to the Board.

Apologies for absence were received from Mr R.T. Gough (President, Football Association of Wales), and Mr D.B. Woolfall (Football Association).

The following Proposals of the Football Association, that the Rules be altered as hereinafter mentioned, were carried: –

RULE I. – This Board shall be called the INTERNATIONAL FOOTBALL ASSOCIATION BOARD. The Football Association, the Scottish Football Association, the Football Association of Wales, the Irish Football Association, and La Fédération Internationale de Football Association, shall each be entitled to send two representatives, who shall constitute the Board.

RULE IV: – The Board shall meet annually, on the Second Saturday in June. The meetings shall be held in rotation, in England, Scotland, Wales, Ireland, and Paris, at the invitation of each Association in order of seniority. The invitation for the year 1913 shall be given by Ireland, and for 1914 by The Federation Internationale de Football Association. One of the representatives of the Association convening the meeting shall preside, and the other shall act as Secretary.

RULE VI: – Business shall not be proceeded with at any meeting unless Four Associations are represented.

RULE VII: – Alterations in the Laws of the Game shall only be made at the Annual Meeting in June, and no alteration shall be adopted unless agreed to by at least four-fifths of the representatives present and voting.

RULE VIII: – Omit the word 'four' in the eighth line.

RULE IX: – The decisions of the Board shall be at once binding on all the Associations, and no alterations in the Laws of the Game shall be made by any Association until the same shall have been passed by this Board.

The following Proposal submitted by The Scottish Football Association was unanimously carried.

1. That the English, Scottish, Welsh and Irish Associations petition Parliament to take measures to repress 'Ready Money Football Coupon Betting.'

2. It was further decided that The Football Association take up the matter and circularize Members of Parliament for them to support the measure.

A vote of thanks was tendered the [*sic*] Chairman for presiding.

(Signed) T. ROBBINS,

The Football Association of Wales,

Acting Secretary.

Themes to explore:

1. The formality of the document: its structure, its language, its legalistic and bureaucratic nature.

2. The power relations within football that it reveals.

3. The dissemination of football at the time.

4. The document as part of a series.

▶ 6.5 Other organisations' records

Governments, clubs, and governing bodies are, and have been, important forces in the development of sport, so the primary sources that such bodies have generated are vital for sports history. However, it would be misleading to suggest that these are the only kinds of organisations that have shaped sport over time, and we should briefly consider some others. These are educational institutions, religious organisations, political organisations, and pressure groups.

Schools, college, and universities have been key movers in the history of sport. Organised play and games have long been valued in the educational curricula of many societies, which has given us a variety of primary sources of record and policy. Philosophical treatises on pedagogy, correspondence and syllabus documents from English schools in the nineteenth century, and the official reports and minutes of thousands of school and university sports clubs comprise this disparate archive. In many cases, this evidence is useful not just for research into the history of sport within any given establishment, it can also take us back to the roots of bigger strands in sports history. These include the codification of sports – such as basketball in the YMCA Training School in Springfield in 1891 or football in Cambridge University in 1846 – or the formation of clubs that outgrew their scholastic foundation. Survival has often depended upon the schools and universities themselves, so those institutions with the resources to devote to archiving tend to be better represented than others: but many schools maintained formal logbooks from an early stage, and many of these have been transferred to record offices. As with governmental records, educational ones are excellent ways into the mentality of sports' providers in the past. The planners' concerns about the development of the children or young people in their charge were indicative of their wider philosophies about the nature and role of physical exercise in education.

Religion has, in some cases, overlapped with education in sports history, and many religious organisations – such as churches, chapels, mosques, synagogues, temples, and their educational wings – have taken a formal role in developing sports clubs. This work has left behind evidence of record and policy. We can use such material to gain information on the geographical, and crucially the cultural, spread of sports in our given society, information that is particularly useful if we are studying multicultural and multifaith societies, such as the UK since 1945, or India for any period in its modern history. Different religions' attitudes towards their members playing certain sports on certain days are recoverable from official records, as is evidence of leagues and competitions on either intra-faith or more accessible lines. As with schools, such material can take us into the birth of bigger history, while also giving us a way into the social and cultural history of the periods we are studying.

As we noted in the discussion of governments above, structural political involvement in sport has a longer history in some political traditions than it does in others, but the roughly simultaneous emergence of modern sport and modern party politics has ensured that there has always been some common ground. Many political organisations have formally promoted sport for its members, such as the socialist Clarion cycling clubs of late Victorian Britain, dedicated to fellowship and healthy exercise, the Turner societies of nineteenth-century Germany, with strong links to nationalist parties, and the international Communist-backed Workers' Olympiads of the interwar period. The motivations behind these different examples varied, as did their success: but in each case, the primary evidence of record and policy alerts us to the links that existed between political ideology and spare time activities.

In all of these cases, you need to be aware of any organisation's nature and history when researching its sports-related records. In some cases, sport was central to the organisation's activities, as in the pressure groups based on workers' sport, access to the land, or the maintenance of hunting. In others, such as schools and religious organisations, sport was at best only a small part of the body's remit, and in some cases only a marginal feature. Sport's overall role will thus have had an influence on the quantity of relevant primary evidence, and on its chances of survival. Where material has survived, its current location varies. Some organisations, such as private schools and universities, maintain their own archives; in other cases, and in a fashion similar to that noted above for some sports clubs, records have been taken over by professional archives.

▶ **6.6 Private papers**

Sports historians also use private papers, the personal archives left by individuals. Depending on the individual's role and career, these could fit into any of the categories above, so their disparate nature forces us to consider them here. Although private papers are not bound to have the kind of official status that organisations' archives have, they can still contain evidence of policy and record, particularly when they contain diaries and correspondence. The scope of the sources here is massive, so let us consider a few examples. Pierre de Coubertin, the founder of the International Olympic Committee (IOC), left his papers to the IOC; American Olympic administrator Avery Brundage's papers are in the University of Illinois' archives. Some figures from other walks of life, such as British politician Philip Noel-Baker, left large amounts of sports-related material in their private papers. Moreover, much can be discovered about sport in the past from the letters and diaries of individual observers, people who were not directly or professionally involved in sport, but who recorded their impressions of it in their own private writings. Famous diarists such as Samuel Pepys, John Evelyn, and Fanny Burney all mention sport, for example, and their texts can be used as first-hand accounts. To use this material effectively, you will need to know about the organisations within which the authors were working or, if they were purely private, some biographical information about them. You also need to be patient, as holdings are sometimes split between different collections, and indexing is not always as effective as it could be. However, such papers can provide so much detail on what sport was like in the past that they are essential sources for sports historians.

Activity 4: Extract from Fanny Burney's diary, August 1773[12]

We are just going to Tingmouth Races, which, indeed, are to be held in sight of our house. We hope for very good sport . . .

The sport began by an Ass Race. There were sixteen of the long eared tribe; some of them really ran extremely well; others were truly ridiculous; but all of them diverting. Next followed a Pig Race. This was certainly cruel, for the poor animal had his tail cut to within the length of an inch, and then that inch was soaped. It was then let loose and made run. It was to be the property of the man who could catch it by the tail; which after many ridiculous attempts was found to be impossible, it was so very slippery. Therefore the candidates concluded this day's sport by running for it themselves. The great *Sweep Stakes* of the asses were half-a guinea; the second prize a crown, and the third half-a-crown. However, the whole of it was truly laughable.

The next Race day was not till Friday, which day was also destined to a grand Cricket Match. Mr Rishton is a very good player; and there is an excellent ground on the Den. . . . The cricket players dined on the Green, where they had a booth erected, and a dinner from the Globe, the best Inn here, to which Mrs Rishton added a *hash*, which Mr T. Mills assured her was most excellent, and Mr Hurrel himself eat three times of it! And that, he remarked, indisputably proved its goodness!

The Cricket Match was hardly over before the Tingmouth games began. All that was to be done this second day was Wrestling, a most barbarous diversion, and which I could not look on, and would not have gone to if I had not feared being thought affected. A ring was formed for the combatants by a rope railing, from which we stood to see the sport!! The wrestler was to conquer twice, one opponent immediately after another, to entitle himself to the prize. A strong labouring man came off victorious in the first battles; but while his shins were yet bleeding, he was obliged to attack another. The hat (their gauntlet) was thrown by a servant of Mr Colburn's. He was reckoned by the judges an admirable wrestler, and he very fairly beat his adversary . . .

The Tingmouth Games concluded the day after with a Rowing Match between the women of Shaldon, a fishing town on the other side of the Ting, and the fair ones of this place. For all the men are at Newfoundland every summer, and all laborious work is done by the women, who have a strength and hardiness which I have never seen before in our race . . .

The women rowed with astonishing dexterity and quickness. There were five boats of them. The prizes which they won were shifts with pink ribbands. Games such as these, Mr Crispen says, ought to make future events be dated as universally from Tingmothiads as former ones were from Olympiads.

Themes to explore:

1. The variety and nature of the sports and activities involved.

2. Evidence of social patronage

3. Evidence of gender roles and expectations.

4. The author's writing style

▶ 6.7 Conclusion

The types of sources covered in this chapter are all prominent in sports history, and the discussions and extracts will have given you a sense of the potential evidence base for certain kinds of research. In Chapter 7, we shall continue this theme with a consideration of some other types of evidence.

7 Primary Sources in Sports History 2

In this chapter, we will look at more types of primary sources that sports historians use: advertising materials, polemical sources, creative literature, fine art and photography, feature films, ephemera and artefacts, maps, and retrospective sources (memoirs and interviews). The chapter follows the same structure as Chapter 6.

▶ 7.1 Advertising materials

Advertising has a long history, as providers of goods and services have used public places – including walls, newspapers and magazines, radio and television broadcasts, published trade directories and telephone listings, and the sponsorship of sports and arts events – to get their brands and products widely known. The range and variety of advertisements means that they are available to historians of many subjects and periods, including sports historians. Advertisements for sports products provide us with visual evidence of what sport looked like, albeit in idealised ways. The countless newspaper and magazines advertisements for everything from golf balls to sports bras that have appeared from the late nineteenth century onwards give us straightforward information on appearance, costs, manufacturing technologies, and distribution networks. More subtle readings of such materials can also provide evidence of the kind of people who played particular sports, and of such aspects of the period as aspiration and idealisation. This can be seen in many advertisements, such as the late nineteenth-century posters for various brands of bicycle that showed fashionable young men and women cycling together in idyllic rural settings. In addition to advertisements for sports products themselves, many advertisers have used images from sport to sell unrelated or peripheral items, and these advertisements can also tell us about the appearance and the image of sport at the time in question. Food and drink manufacturers have often used sporting images to suggest the health-giving properties of their goods, as in the nineteenth-century posters for the beef extract Bovril featuring women golfers, while advertisements for luxury goods, such as Rolex watches, have often featured sports with a matching image, such as polo or motor racing.

In addition to advertisements, sports historians can get plenty of useful information from trade directories and similar publications, such as commercial telephone directories.[1] In the UK, these annual publications emerged in the eighteenth century as a way in which tradesmen, manufacturers, and professionals in the new cities could advertise their services. They also tend to provide local information, with listings – often street by street – of businesses, public buildings, sports grounds, place of worship, pubs, and homes. When used in conjunction with contemporary maps, such sources can help you build up a detailed profile of particular communities and areas, which is essential if you want to place a sports club in its specific neighbourhood context. Such publications survived until the 1950s, gradually being replaced by telephone directories such as *Yellow Pages* and, subsequently, Internet-based trade directories. In all cases, you need to remember the advertising motive behind the source's existence, while using it is a relatively objective account of communities' composition.

Advertisements are not always easy to read as historical evidence. As with all other sources, you need to do the contextual work before you can make sense of them. In addition, you need to develop the skills of visual analysis, as many of them rely heavily on still or moving images for their impact. Here, wider reading around the image is necessary to find out what the advertisers wished to connote by such features of an advertisement as the clothes being worn, and the landscapes in which events are depicted. These would all have been apparent to contemporary viewers – the all-important primary audience – without the kind of research that we need to undertake. The same rule applies when real sportsmen and women are used in an advertisement. You may recognise Tiger Woods selling a Buick or David Beckham selling Pepsi Cola and know the kind of lifestyle with which they are associated; but you may not immediately get the same meanings in an 1870s poster for Colmans Mustard featuring the cricketer W.G. Grace. You also need to balance visual and written or spoken aspects of any advertisement, and be able to separate the factual content of how much items cost from the implied content of what might happen to you if you use Brand X. Access is also an issue. Some forms of advertisement are easily accessible to researchers, particularly those that appeared in newspapers and magazines, and the small number that have been reproduced in postcard form by such organisations as the Opie Collection, the London Transport Museum, and various sporting museums and halls of fame. However, original posters are more difficult: their materials were not designed to last for historical scrutiny, and those that do survive are expensive to preserve and store. Some holdings are digitising their advertisements, which will make research easier, but this will always diminish the original impact by reducing the poster's size.

▶ 7.2 Polemical sources

Even the most basic engagement with sports history will have shown you that sport has always been subject to debate and dispute, and there is, as a result, a large amount of primary evidence that we could class as polemical. Such materials are about sides and perspectives, and they should be read by the sports historian as evidence of points of view rather than as objective evidence of what sport was like. Obviously, the nature of polemical sources has varied over time, depending – as with newspapers and advertisements – on such wider factors as technology and literacy rates. They include sermons, books, pamphlets, newspaper editorials and articles, and, more recently, websites dedicated to particular causes. Sports historians can use such sources for a number of reasons. First, and most obviously, we can use them to enhance our understanding of what sport was like in the society under research. Allowing for their inherent subjectivity, we can still learn from such details as how sports were organised, what types of people were involved, and what happened in the sport. Beyond this, we can see the kind of connections that people at the time were making between sport and wider concerns: philosophical, moral, ethical, spiritual, political, economic, and many more. For example, *The Anatomie of Abuses*, written by the sixteenth-century puritan Phillip Stubbes, linked sports such as football and bear-baiting with other activities the author classed as immoral and irreligious, and condemned them as being diversions from both religious purity and economic well-being. Polemics, even those that centre on sport, have never been just about sport, so we should use them to get a sense of the wider issues at stake in our historical society's discourses on such diverse issues as money, morality, humanitarianism, religion, and class relations. Such concerns are particularly evident in the polemical sources from all sides in the long-running debate over the treatment of animals in sport: from Henry Salt's 1892 calls for the recognition of animals' rights to the Countryside

Alliance's more recent claims on hunting's significance to the rural economy, we can see how polemical sources on sport always connect to the wider context.[2]

Many sources of this type are widely available to modern researchers. Many books and pamphlets are available in critical editions and on the Internet, while collected editions of sermons, pamphlets, and articles on a range of issues from ramblers' rights to opposition to gambling are also in the public domain. Recent organisations, such as the League Against Cruel Sports and the Countryside Alliance, have websites that can take you into their literature and propaganda, although you need to remember that content will frequently change, and not every website provides its own archive. Locating such materials can be time-consuming, particularly if they are available only in copyright libraries, but judicious use of published sports historians' bibliographies, and an open ear to debates in any of the sources you read, can provide you with key names and references to follow up in your period. When using them, you will need to conduct appropriate contextual research on the authors and their affiliations. Look out for any obvious clues on the positions taken, which can range from an article's title to the organisation that has published the text. For example, it does not require much historical imagination to work out the orientation of such a polemical source as an article entitled 'Gambling and the Bible' published in the Florida Baptist Witness.[3] When dealing with such materials, it is vitally important for you to understand the contemporary meanings of the words used, as anachronistic assumptions could lead you to misunderstand the argument. You also need to remember at all times that such sources were designed to persuade: their style, structure, and tone will all have been dedicated to inciting contemporary readers to action.

Activity 1: Extracts from Phillip Stubbes, *The Anatomie of Abuses* (1583)[4]

Please note that I have not changed the punctuation or spelling, except to render 'f' as 's' and 'v' as 'u' where pronunciation dictates.
On bear-baiting, pp. 177–78

> These Hethnicall exercyses upon the Sabaoth day, which the Lord hath consecrate to holy uses, for the glory of his Name, and our spirituall comfort, are not in any respect tolerable, or to be suffered. For is not the baiting of a Bear, besides that it is a filthie, stinking, and lothsome game, a daungerous & perilous exercise? Wherein a man is in daunger of his life every minut of an houre; which thing, though it weare not so, yet

what exercise is this meet for any Christian? What Christen heart can take pleasure to see une poore beast to rent, teare, and kill another, and all for his foolish pleasure? And although they be bloody beasts to mankind, & seeke his destruction, yet we are not to abuse them, for his sake who made them, & whose creatures they are. For, notwithstanding that they be evill to us, & thirst after our blood, yet are thei good creatures in their own nature & kind, & made to set foorth the glorie & magnificence of the great God, & for our use; & therefore for his sake not to be abused.

On cockfighting, hawking, and hunting, pp. 180–81.

Besides these exercises, thei flock, thick & three fold, to the cockfeights, an exercise nothing inferiour to the rest, wher nothing is used but swering, forswering, deceit, fraude, collusion, cosenage, scoulding, railing, conuitious talking, feighting, brawling, quarrelling, drinking, whooring; &, which is worst of all, robbing of one an other of their goods, & that not by direct, but indirect means & attempts: & yet to blaunch & set out these mischiefs withal (as though they were vertues) thei have their appointed daies & set howrs, when these divelries must be exercised. They have houses erected to the purpose, flags & engines hanged out, to give notice of it to others, and proclamation goes out to proclaim the fame, to th' end that many may come to the dedication of this solemne feast of mischief: the Lord supplant them! And as for hawking & hunting upon the sabaoth day, it is an exercise upon that day no lesse unlawful than the other; For no man ought to spend any day of his life, much lesse every day in his life, as many do, in such vaine & ydle pastimes: wherefore let Gentlemen take heed; for, be sure, accounts must be given at the day of judgement for every minut of time, both how they have spent it, & in what exercises. And let them be sure no more libertie is given to them to misspend an howre, or one iote of the Lord his goods, than is given to the poorest and meanest person that liveth upon the face of the earth. I never read of any, in the volume of the sacred scripture, that was a good man and a Hunter.

Themes to explore:

1. Phillip Stubbes' political and religious views.

2. The political and religious climate of late sixteenth-century England.

3. The popularity and distribution of bear-baiting, cock-fighting, hawking, and hunting in late sixteenth-century England.

4. The accuracy or otherwise of Stubbes' claims about the 'abuses' that went on around these sports.

▶ 7.3 Creative literature

Creative writing, such as literature and song lyrics, may seem at first glance to be an unlikely type of primary source for sports history. Its creative nature means that it is not bound to be 'true' in a positivist view of evidence. Something that an author had made up for artistic and commercial reasons, it could be argued, does not have the same kind of veracity as a newspaper report or a parliamentary debate. Against this, we can argue that while such sources are not obliged to tell *the* truth, they can tell *a* truth which can be useful to the historian. Literature and songs can capture impressions of what sport was like at the time that you are studying, and can, when used alongside other sources, help us to locate sport in its social contexts. There are many examples we could use to illustrate this. David Storey's 1960 novel *This Sporting Life*, for example, provides a vivid picture of the social setting for 1960s rugby league, and provides ways into the gender and social politics of the sport at the time.[5] E.M. Forster's novel *A Room with a View* (1908) and John Betjeman's poems, such as 'Pot Pourri from a Surrey Garden' (1940), give first-hand accounts of lawn tennis amongst the upper-middle classes.[6] Baseball has provided the setting for a number of American novels of high critical standing, including Bernard Malamud's *The Natural* of 1952 and Philip Roth's *The Great American Novel* of 1973.[7] Many Victorian poets made links between sport, public school spirit, and military service, encapsulated perfectly in Henry Newbolt's 'Vitaï Lampada' of 1897:

> The sand of the desert is sodden red,-
>
> Red with the wreck of a square that broke;-
> The Gatling's jammed and the Colonel dead,
> And the regiment blind with dust and smoke.
> The river of death has brimmed his banks,
> And England's far, and Honour a name,
> But the voice of a schoolboy rallies the ranks:
> 'Play up! play up! and play the game!'[8]

Popular songs can also be studied for the light they shed on sporting heroes and cultures. Examples include 'Take Me to the Ball Game', British music-hall songs such as Marie Lloyd's 'Salute My Bicycle', calypso celebrations of cricketers such as The Mighty Sparrow's 'Sir Garfield Sobers' and Lord Kitchener's 'The Cricket Song', and indie pop songs on football themes, such as Half Man Half Biscuit's 'All I Want for Christmas is the Dukla Prague Away Kit'. These can all be used as evidence of the culture, language, and heroes of sport at the time they were created. These few examples suggest the scope and range of this type of source material across genres, which encompasses novels, short stories, plays, poems, comics, and songs.

It is difficult to generalise across this range of media and periods, but none of these artistic products cover sport by accident: in each case, the author must have seen in sport the potential to be the vehicle for his or her wider theme. The theme may have been celebration, humour, satire, social concern, or the piece may have been created for aesthetic or simply commercial reasons. Sport's ability to convey narratives of triumph and disaster, joy and despair, winning and losing, and its capacity to carry stories about class, identity, and the human spirit have made it popular amongst creative writers throughout history. As such, they can give sports historians a sense of the past's flavour: not just the obvious aspects like what it looked like (accessible through descriptive passages in the works) and how it sounded (accessible through speech and language patterns), but also such aspects as the beliefs, attitudes, and mores of the time under investigation. If we take as a starting point the assumption that people who create artistic pieces want them to reflect and embody their way of looking at the world, then these subjective aspects of the time will always come through.

Creative sources are widely accessible today, and following up on other historians' usage of them – such as Jeff Hill's work on popular literature, Richard Fotheringham's analysis of sporting plays, and Michael Oriard's work on sport in American fiction – can take you into whole new areas of reading.[9] University, public, and copyright libraries have huge holdings of creative writing, and many whole texts are available online. Obviously, you will need specialised skills to make the most of them. First, remember that the usual rules about context apply: you must locate any creative piece in its exact setting, taking account of where and when it was written, and who the author was. David Storey's rugby league stories have a sense of authenticity, for example, that would have been hard to capture if Storey himself had not played professionally, and you need to find this kind of information out about your writers. It is also worthwhile finding out about the piece's original reception and later reputation. Second, take some time to study the genre of the piece. Is it a popular novel (such as Dick Francis' horse racing books) or a more artistic piece (such as Philip Roth's *The Great American Novel*)? Was it written as a poem or a song: and, if the latter, what was the music like? What were the key trends in that genre at the time of publication? Third, you need to work with the piece's actual content, studying its form (such as the narrative voice in a novel, or the rhyme scheme in a poem), its language, and its subject. Taken together, these approaches can help you get a sense of how a sport was perceived and interpreted at the time under review.

Activity 2: 'Take Me Out to the Ball Game', lyrics by Jack Norworth, music by Albert Von Tilzer (1908 version)[10]

Katie Casey was baseball mad.
Had the fever and had it bad;
Just to root for the home town crew,
Ev'ry sou Katie blew.
On a Saturday, her young beau
Called to see if she'd like to go,
To see a show but Miss Kate said,
"No, I'll tell you what you can do."

"Take me out to the ball game,
Take me out with the crowd.
Buy me some peanuts and cracker jack,
I don't care if I never get back,
Let me root, root, root for the home team,
If they don't win it's a shame.
For it's one, two, three strikes, you're out,
At the old ball game."

Katie Casey saw all the games,
Knew the players by their first names;
Told the umpire he was wrong,
All along good and strong.
When the score was just two to two,
Katie Casey knew what to do,
Just to cheer up the boys she knew,
She made the gang sing this song:

"Take me out to the ball game,
Take me out with the crowd.
Buy me some peanuts and cracker jack,
I don't care if I never get back,
Let me root, root, root for the home team,
If they don't win it's a shame.
For it's one, two, three strikes, you're out,
At the old ball game."

Themes to explore:

1. The popularity and distribution of baseball in early twentieth-century America.

2. The gender relations embodied in the song.

3. Gender, social, and commercial aspects of American urban society at the time.

4. The value of the lyrics alone as a source, and the role of the song's music.

5. The song's afterlife.

► 7.4 Fine art and photography

People have been making visual representations of human activity for longer than they have been writing: for many periods, visual evidence along with artefacts and other archaeological materials are all that historians have to go on. With the recent growth of cultural history and art history, historians have become more adept at using such materials as evidence, and sports historians have been able to exploit this type of material for information about the past. From Roman mosaics, for example, we have gained insight on the appearance of gladiators and their equipment and fighting styles. From classical Greek statues and illustrated ceramics, we have a sense of what gymnasts, runners, jumpers, and fighters looked like. Medieval illuminated manuscripts, such as books of hours and prayer books, sometimes included images of people at play. Some artists from the medieval period to the present have treated sport as a subject, either as a major theme or as a background setting in paintings of everyday life. Examples across this period include Aert van der Neer's 'Golfers and Skaters near a Village' (c.1648), John Robertson Reid's 'A Country Cricket Match' (1878), Pablo Picasso's 'The Swimmer' (1934), Andy Warhol's 'Baseball' (1962), and Duane Hanson's 'Football Player' (1981). Even making allowances for artists' aesthetic intentions which may have idealised their representations, or concentrated only on specific aspects such as movement, conflict, or landscape, such works provide evidence of styles of play, patronage, clothing, equipment, sporting landscapes, and the geographical distribution of sports. Sporting portraiture has a particular value here. Commissioned portraits such as Oswald Birley's 'David Lord Burghley (as a Cambridge Blue)' (1926) and Ray Richardson's 'Lennox Lewis' (1993) give us the kind of visual clues about sport mentioned above. Moreover, such paintings by their existence provide evidence of the fame, popularity, wealth, and success of the sportsmen and women who have been painted.[11]

Individual paintings and statues are accessible in the collections that house them, and it is worth taking the effort to see them in their proper formats if you are using them as evidence. The reproduction of a painting such as Frith's *The Derby Day* (1858) in a book, for example, cannot really do justice to a canvas that measures 40 × 88 inches. However, visits to galleries may not always be possible. Art history books for the period you are studying, or *catalogues raisonée* of individual artists, will provide you with both images and details about their production, while websites such as Artchive and Grove Art Online will provide you with not only images of paintings but also statues and works in other media.[12] For effective analysis, you will need to study the form of any visual evidence and learn its traditions and devices. Approaching a medieval manuscript which includes a picture of a monk playing bowls, for example, as if it were attempting to be an accurate portrayal of an individual will be misleading. Instead, you need to understand the idiom, and use the image as a representation of sport. This is also true of modern art that has covered sport: as photographers can deliver realism and authentic action, so painters have concentrated on the essence of sport, on representing the action, the personalities, the aesthetics, and the settings of sport. This is clear in such works as Paul Klee's modernist *Runner at the Goal.*

The development of photography in the nineteenth century created a medium with more obvious authenticity than the other arts, particularly as its technology improved to allow for capturing live action. Its mass availability and, from the 1930s, mass consumption has made it the most democratic form of visual evidence, and the most plentiful. This type of visual evidence for sport is thus plentiful in family collections, club archives, newspapers and magazines, and art collections. All of these forms are valuable as evidence for the sports historian. Across the range, they can be used for evidence of what sport, its players, its spectators, and its facilities and equipment looked like in the past. High art photography, such as Julian Germain's *In Soccer Wonderland* of 1994,[13] can give us the same clues as fine art mentioned above, while formal club and school team photographs give us incomparable snapshots of real people who played sport. Reportage photography gives us direct representation of real sporting action, and allows us to see what some legendary moments in sport looked like. Roger Bannister breaking the tape at Iffley Road in 1954, Muhammad Ali standing over the prone Sonny Liston in 1965, Bob Beamon's long-jump at the 1968 Mexico City Olympics, sailor Ellen MacArthur as she broke the record for a solo non-stop circumnavigation of the world in 2005: these are iconic moments known widely through split second photographs that are worth analysis. At a grassroots level, family snapshots of people competing in school or voluntary sport, completing marathons or playing games on holidays are all potentially useful as evidence, giving us images of clothing, equipment, and the balance between formal and informal sport.

Activity 3: Sport in fine art

Using Grove Art Online (http://www.groveart.com), Mark Harden's Artchive (http://www.artchive.com), or the homepages of the galleries and museums named below, find images of the following artworks.

1. Foundry Painter (attributed), *Red-Figured Cup with Pankratiasts, boxers, and other athletes*, c.500–475 BC (The British Museum, London)

2. Pieter Bruegel the Elder, *Winter Landscape with Skaters and Bird Trap*, 1565 (Musées Royaux des Beaux-Arts, Brussels)

3. Francis Nicolson, *Edinburgh from Bruntsfield Links*, late eighteenth/early nineteenth century (Victoria and Albert Museum, London)

4. Georges Seurat, *Bathers at Asnieres* (*Une baignade, Asniéres*), 1884 (National Gallery, London)

5. Henri Rousseau, *The Football Players* (*Les Joueurs de Football*), 1908 (Guggenheim Museum, New York City)

6. George Bellows, *Tennis Tournament*, 1920 (National Gallery of Art, Washington DC)

7. El Lissitzky, *Runner in the City*, c.1926 (Metropolitan Museum of Art, New York City)

8. Max Beckmann, *Rugby Players*, 1929 (Wilhem-Lehmbruck-Museum, Duisburg)

9. David Hockney, *A Bigger Splash*, 1967 (Tate Gallery, London)

10. Alex Katz, *The Swimmer*, 1974 (National Museum of American Art, Smithsonian Institute, Washington DC)

Themes to explore:

1. Realism versus impressionism in their representation of sport.

2. The environments in which sport is shown taking place.

3. Representations of gender and social roles.

4. Clothing and equipment.

5. Each artwork in its own cultural historical context.

▶ 7.5 Feature films

Sport has always proved popular with feature film makers. Sport's inherent action, and its host of possible narratives, has made it a rich source material in many countries' film industries. Examples include Robert Wise's *Someone Up There Likes Me* (1956), Hugh Hudson's *Chariots of Fire* (1981), Martin Scorsese's *Raging Bull* (1980), Peter Weir's *Gallipoli* (1981), and Ashutosh Gowariker's *Lagaan: Once Upon a Time in India* (2001). As with novels about sport, the quality varies greatly here, from the critically respected *Raging Bull* to the widely derided *When Saturday Comes* or the *Mighty Ducks* franchise. In general, such films attempt to be authentic within the constraints of the form, as part of their appeal is based on their veracity amongst informed viewers. This should mean that they can be useful as way into the sport at the time the film is set. A good example of this is Lindsay Anderson's *This Sporting Life*, where the rugby league action is rendered realistically, and where the staged film sequences involving actors are interspersed with real footage of crowds at Wakefield Trinity RFC. However, this type of evidence can never be as reliable as news film, as feature film-makers have always had to work at one remove from real sport due to their reliance on actors and artificial scenes. The frequent use of slow-motion in such films not only is a dramatic device, but also helps to disguise the speeds at which actors are capable of moving in relation to the sports professionals they are playing. In this sense, it is crucial for you to approach feature films as evidence in the same way that you would approach novels: as highly fictionalised, impressionistic pieces that can tell you something about what sport looked like and how it was perceived at the time of production. Some feature films are historical: they deal with subjects from an earlier period. *Chariots of Fire* – made in the 1980s, but set in the 1920s – is a famous example of this. In these cases, it is crucial to avoid the temptation of treating it as a primary source for the 1920s. Not only do such films make historical mistakes, they also deal extremely selectively with the material. In the case of *Chariots of Fire*, for example, the pre-Olympic race between Abrahams and Liddell that is so crucial in setting up the two athletes' rivalry never happened, but it served the purpose of the film's narrative to create it. So, rather than use such films to find out about the past they portray, use them as primary sources of the time in which they were made, and see what they can tell you about the concerns and preoccupations of the society in which they were made.

Home video and DVD ownership and film supply networks, and the growth of multi-channel television, mean that many feature films are now easily accessible for research; and the viewer's ability to freeze and replay scenes makes them easy to analyse. However, many films, particularly from the early days of cinema when film stock was fragile, have not survived, so researchers here face similar problems to their colleagues working with other forms of evidence for which the materials now available are only a fraction of what was created. Analysing feature films historically requires some special skills. You need to read them in the context of wider trends in the film industry, such as *This Sporting Life* being part of the kitchen sink film movement of the early 1960s. You also need to locate them politically and culturally in their time and place of production. *Rocky IV* (1985), for example, is obviously about US–Soviet relations in the 1980s, being played out in microcosm through boxing. A knowledge of some technical aspects of film-making will also help your analysis, as it will allow you to note such aspects as camera angles, lighting techniques, and sound quality, all of which have a bearing on the film's value as a source. Finally, as with fine art sources discussed above, you need to be prepared to balance feature films against other sources so that you can both spot errors and gain insights. They are challenging sources to use: but their potential value as evidence of how stories about sport were being told in a high profile media at the time you are studying should make the challenge worthwhile.

► 7.6 Ephemera and artefacts

As well as documents, newspapers, films, and the other types of sources listed above, sport has generated many other types of evidence that we can class as ephemera, 'the minor transient documents of everyday life'.[14] For sports history, such a category can include such items as matchday programmes, tickets, scorecards, autograph books, and packaging of sports equipment. In addition, artefacts such as equipment (balls, bats, racquets, clubs, starting blocks, and thousands of others) and sports clothing can be used as evidence. Such items can tell us a great deal about sport. Programmes, for example, provide evidence of players' careers, supporters' cultures and activities, playing styles, commercial and economic information, and clubs as communities, while autograph books tell us about fame and fandom. Clothing and equipment allow us to get a physical sense of what it was like to play sport in the past: there is nothing like feeling the weight of a nineteenth-century tennis racket, or the material of a 1920s swimming costume, to give you a sense of how different those sports must have been for participants then compared to now. The growth of interest in such items, both as collectibles and as historical sources, is reflected in such books as Robert McElroy and Grant MacDougall's *Football Memorabilia*, Simon Inglis' *A Load of Old Balls*, and Frank Slocum's *Classic Baseball Cards: The Golden Years, 1886–1956*.[15]

Typically, sporting ephemera is abundant in family collections, albeit often in a disorganised way, and it is increasingly being collected professionally by museums. Private collectors are also involved, as witness the trading in such items through formal auction houses such as Christie's and Sotheby's, online through eBay, and through memorabilia fairs and trading meetings in all major sports. However, it is difficult to quantify the volume of such materials, and, outside museums, access can be difficult due to the private nature of collections. However, this is the type of material that you can often come across serendipitously while carrying out other research, such as oral history or newspaper work. Analysis of such sources needs to take account of their physical nature and their original purpose, and of the materials and processes that went into making them. Use visual evidence of such items being used, such as paintings, photographs, newspapers, or films, or, if possible, talk to older people who may have used them. This process will help you to understand the objects more fully, and thus use them as evidence in an informed way.

▶ 7.7 Maps and landscapes

No historian of any subject can get away without using maps. They are essential to our understanding of every aspect of human history, from trade patterns to diplomacy, from transport and industrial development to war and exploration. When it comes to sports history, historical maps can help us to understand a number of aspects. International maps can help us to trace the dissemination of sports across the world, allowing us to connect political, military, and commercial links to the cities and countries through which sports spread. The spread of cricket in the nineteenth century, for example, becomes far clearer if the dates of matches are read alongside a map of the British Empire. Local and national maps are similarly essential, allowing us to read a sports site – a cricket ground, a bowling green, a bearpit, a racetrack, or any other areas – as part of a specific landscape. Maps can show us the distances between transport networks and the places where sports were played, the interrelationship between the development of sports sites and the development of other parts of communities, and the cultural import- ance of sports sites, judged by their centrality or marginality. Finally, maps can give a sense of how landscapes that were managed for sport looked: hunting areas, with their coverts; managed fishing lakes, with dams or sluices; and ski slopes, maintained for the benefit of winter sports enthusiasts. Overall, when we remember how important the geographical context is to understand any sport in history, the role of maps becomes paramount.

Map-making and cartography have become increasingly sophistic- ated over time, and you need to be aware of the contemporary methods and styles of maps for the period you are studying. Scientific detail that you would expect from modern maps cannot be assumed: distances measured in 'paces' or hills drawn from side-on views rather than represented in contour lines are two examples of this. Make sure you find out why a particular map was made, and who commissioned it, so that you have a context for it as a source. It is also important to compare maps of the same area over time, as this can show continuity and change in sports usage. For international and national mapping, there are many useful historical atlases available.[16] When using these, remember how quickly things can change, ranging from an international border being moved as a result of a treaty to a new railway being built between two towns, and be ready to do some wider reading to understand and visualise such changes. If you are researching local sports history, then use your local historical resources to locate and analyse maps. In the UK, these will usually be in county and city record office and local studies collections in libraries. Through these, you will be able to handle old maps, and should be able to build up a reliable picture of the community over a period spanning the centuries.[17] There are also a number of websites that provide historical maps, which are valuable if you are unable to get to a particular library, and which enable you to make instant comparisons across time and place.[18] Make sure you take account of scales, frequency of revisions, and any other factors that will help you interpret the map. Finally, there is no substitute for field walking to bring historical maps to life. Exploring on foot the areas that have been used for sport in the past can give you a sense of place that no other kind of historical research in this area can bring, similar to the sense that military historians can get from walking battlefields. Being in the real locations gives you more tangible information, such as the size and scale of playing areas, and the local terrain and topography. Such visits can also lead you to commemorative artefacts, such as street names, statues, and plaques, all of which are both evidence of the old sports use and important pieces of public history.

Activity 4: Bacon's plan of St Marylebone, London, c.1895[19]

Themes to explore:

1. The exact location of Lord's cricket ground and the nature and social profile of its immediate environment.

2. The presence and distribution of other sporting sites shown on the map, such as the lake and the Toxophilite Society's grounds inside Regents Park, and the proximity of transport infrastructure.

3. The interrelationship between developed and open spaces in the map as a whole, and the implications of this relationship for sport.

4. Compare this map with others of the same area from other periods to see evidence of continuity and change in sport use.

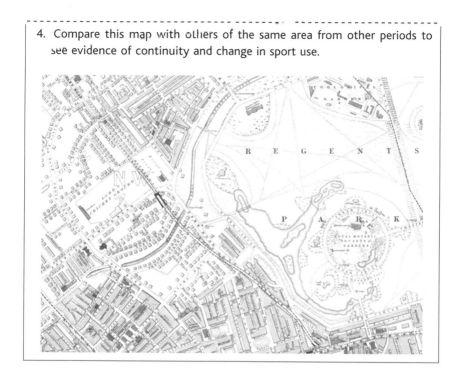

► 7.8 Retrospective sources

All of the types of evidence discussed above can be seen as primary if they were created in the period you are researching. However, many historians also use sources that cannot be classed as primary in such pure terms, but are not quite secondary sources either. These are sources that have been created after the time being studied, but are based on the creator's first-hand observation of the events that happened at the time. When using such sources, you need to be sure to research the time in which the source was made – when an autobiography was written, for example, or when an interview was made – as this will have a bearing on its representation of the past. However, when used with caution, these sources can add a personal dimension to our understanding of the past.

7.8.1 Memoirs and autobiographies

The most accessible type of evidence here for the sports historian is the published memoir or autobiography. There are thousands of such books published annually, and historians of all disciplines use them for the light they shed on how well-placed individuals – soldiers, politicians, actors, and so on – viewed the events through which they have lived. There is also a growing body of autobiographies by people who were not famous until they wrote, but whose stories of everyday life or extraordinary events have made them well known: Frank McCourt's *Angela's Ashes* and its sequels are examples of this. In sport, too, there is no shortage of this literature. Since the early days of sporting celebrity in the nineteenth century, there has been a market for first-person accounts by the great players. The supply of such accounts multiplied during the course of the twentieth century, as more people became nationally and internationally famous for their sport, and players were joined by coaches and administrators, a trend that has continued with sport's growth. It is possible that we are now at saturation point, with thousands of new sporting autobiographies published annually.

These sources are, in general, of great value to the sports historian. For past periods, they are one of the few routes we have to the individual's view of the events that he or she lived through, and his or her role in them. Even for elite sportsmen and women who are still alive at the time of your research, reading an autobiography is a more realistic form of access than an interview. At their best, memoirs can tell us something about the individual's feelings and actions, and they can convey something of the climate of sport at the time. Critical reading can also take you into the individual's world view, particularly useful when you are trying to put their sporting experience into a wider context. Through this filter, you can approach such positions as patriotism, racism, and gender identity. The key element here that makes these works useful is their official nature. They will have either been written by the player himself or herself, or by an approved ghost-writer – usually a trusted journalist – who will base the text on interviews with the subject. This relationship means that what gets written has the approval of the subject. This can make them bland: the anodyne account of professional life, glamour, camaraderie, anecdotes from foreign travels, and complaints about how today's stars are overpaid and under-skilled is typical of this genre across all sports. The official nature also means that many aspects of the performer's life will typically get ignored: anything that shows him or her in a bad light, any law-breaking, or any unflattering personal material rarely has official endorsement. The exceptions to this trend – such as footballer Tony Adams' *Addicted* in which he explored his own alcoholism and prison sentence for drink-driving – are still rarer than the more anodyne books.[20] However, some autobiographers have used the source to criticise certain aspects of their sport. Len Sheckleton's *Clown Prince of Soccer* (1955), for example, is a classic critical memoir, exemplified by its famous chapter on 'The average director's knowledge of football', which consists of a blank page.[21] However, autobiographies have some pitfalls, and you need to recognise these if you want to use them as sources. Most obviously, when using an autobiography you must note when it was published, as that is any text's primary context. A book about sport in the 1950s that was published in the 1990s has to be seen as a product of the 1990s. The concerns, language, and retrospect of that time will have informed the whole exercise. To rely only on the retrospective memoir as evidence of how a player interpreted the past, then, can be misleading. You also need to consider any autobiography's original intended audience and reason for existence. This will invariably take you into financial considerations: sportsmen and women who write autobiographies do so primarily to make some further profit from their fame and fan-base. Finally, you need to consider the role and agenda of the ghost-writer, who is as central to the text as the subject himself or herself. So, for getting myriad accounts of what it was like from people involved, autobiography is an invaluable source: but the issues of authorship, timing, retrospect, and motivations cannot be ignored.

Activity 5: Extract from Harold Larwood with Kevin Perkins, *The Larwood Story*[22]

We batted first, and it was typical Test match play, a little slow if anything, but hard fought. On the second day we had reached a total of 341, Leyland having got 83, Wyatt 78 and Paynter 77. Verity made 45, Tim Wall bowled tenaciously to take 5 for 72 off 34 overs.

The trouble started soon after Australia began its first innings at 3.25 pm. It was another poor start with Fingleton back in the pavilion and only one run on the board. He was out to Allen. Then in the last ball of my second over I hit Woodfull over the heart with one that was just short of a length. He doubled up in pain, and the crowd hooted me wildly. . . .

When I was on my way in to bowl the first ball of my third over to Woodfull, Jardine stopped me in mid stride by clapping his hands, and motioned the field over to the leg side. That was the signal for a tremendous burst of hooting and abuse, but Jardine persisted with the field placing . . . The crowd counted me out as I began each delivery and hooted all the time.

> When Jardine had walked across to me a few minutes earlier, after I hit Woodfull, handed me the ball [*sic*] and said, 'Well bowled, Harold,' Bradman was standing only a few feet away at the bowler's end. I knew what Jardine meant. He was trying to put Bradman off, trying to unsettle him by letting him think the ball was being bowled deliberately to hit the man and that he might get the same. Jardine was a master of the finer points of psychology.
>
> In the same manner, Jardine used to try to bolster the spirits of some of our players, whom he knew to be squeamish about bodyline. As an incoming Australian came out to bat, he would say to those around him: Here comes another 'yellow bastard', meaning that the player was lacking in courage. He usually referred to Bradman as 'that little bastard'.

Themes to explore:

1. The time lag between the events being recounted (1933) and the book being written (1965).

2. The detailed descriptions of events that happened in seconds, and the longer-term analyses of motives and behaviour.

3. The evidence that this extract provides about cricket's culture in the 1930s.

4. The evidence that this extract provides about Anglo-Australian relations, and about social relations in sport.

5. The assumptions that the authors make about the average reader's knowledge of cricket.

6. The relationship between the cricketer Harold Larwood and his collaborator, Kevin Perkins, a professional journalist.

7.8.2 Oral history

Another form of source based on memory is the specially conducted interview. This methodology has grown across all disciplines in history since the 1970s, when the oral history movement emerged. Linked to history from below, oral historians aimed to record and disseminate personal stories of people who may not have been famous or powerful, but whose lives could tell historians about the past. Working methods, family structure, the role of religion in people's lives, even battles as seen by the soldiers in the frontline, all of these themes and many more could be accessed through oral history.[23] Such evidence has much in its favour for sports history. Authorial voice is not in question, as the words are not mediated or rewritten by a ghost-writer. However, the interviewer has a crucial role in wording the questions and thus framing the narrative. Many of the people interviewed would not normally leave a written record behind, so recorded or filmed testimony can save memories and information from dying with the subject. Oral accounts can take us right into the grassroots of a sport, and tell us what it was like at club and individual level. They can thus complement the evidence of record and policy, and the sources of persuasion, discussed above, as they tell us how regular people interacted with their game: what events meant to them, what emotions sport elicited in them, why they got involved with sport. The problem of retrospect applies in oral history just as it does in autobiography. Here, knowledge of what happened later cannot help but influence an account of what an earlier period was like, and the interviewing historian needs to be well informed so as to work with such interpretations. Proving the accuracy of what interviewees say can also be difficult if there are no other corroborative records, so people's natural tendency to exaggerate their happiest and best times and downplay their less flattering conduct can easily go unchecked. However, this is also the case with other, written forms of evidence; and if you approach oral testimony with realistic expectations as a way into people's perceptions of the past that they have lived through, then you can get a lot from it. Overall, you should work with the limitations and make use of oral history, as it is one of the best ways of getting truly original source material. You can use it by researching existing interviews, such as those held in sound archives, or in special collections, such as those commissioned by the Society for American Baseball Research or the Amateur Athletic Foundation of Los Angeles' Olympian Oral Histories project.[24] You could also consider carrying out your own oral history project, which would build on Activity 2 in Chapter 1. This type of research is a great interface between past and present, what oral historian Stephen Caunce calls 'a two-way process, giving something to a contributor as well as the researcher, and requiring something from the collector as well as the contributor'.[25] It allows you as the historian to shape the evidence and to cross examine witnesses to the past in ways that are not possible with written sources. Its human face allows far more direct dialogue across the generations than any amount of newspapers and minute books.

Activity 6: Extract from Margaret Costa's interview with Aileen Riggin, an American swimmer and diver who competed at the 1920 and 1924 Olympic Games. The interview was conducted in November 1994 for the Amateur Athletic Foundation of Los Angeles' Olympic Oral Histories project[26]

Q: OK, I want to go back a little. . . Tell me about your family, were they middle class?

A: My father was in the Navy. He was stationed many places. But when I started to swim, it happened to be in New York. He was stationed at the Brooklyn Navy Yard.

Q: The reason I ask that question is because of the attitudes towards women participating in sports in general.

A: There weren't any sports for women that I can remember. There were no athletic scholarships for sports for women. None of the backups that they have now, the Women's Sports Foundation, for example. . . We had nothing, we started from the ground up. There was no competition. Helen and I competed against each other. It was considered quite remarkable that two girls could do this crawl stroke. We were the first: our group was the first to do it in the club. The Women's Swimming Association of New York.

Q: The Women's Swimming Association of New York, very interesting.

A: We had to compete against the older girls. When competition started, it just began around this time. We would go to different cities to compete, frequently in Philadelphia because it was very close and they had a good team named the Philadelphia Turngemeinde.

Q: The Turners, that may be where a lot of women received their training, through the Turners.

A: Yes, the Turners. Betty Baker, who won the Olympics later, was from that club. But we were great rivals because it was so close and we could just go down and come back on the same day. We used to compete in Buffalo and Chicago, Indianapolis every summer, and Detroit.

Q: OK, you are talking about competing. What was the mode of transport?

A: We went by train. And the trains were wonderful in those days. The sleeping cars were a big treat to us. There were a lot of meets around New York, Long Island, Connecticut, and often Massachusetts. There still weren't any others as young as we were, so we had to compete against the adults. But they weren't so old, they were 17, 18, the oldest would be about 25.

1. The time lag between the events being recounted (c.1917–19) and the interview taking place (1994), and Riggin's age at the time of the interview.

2. The level of detail in Riggin's account.

3. Costa's role in deciding the line of questioning: her aims, her agendas, and her interests.

4. The role of nostalgia and hindsight in Riggin's account.

5. The evidence that this interview can supply about the culture of women's swimming in the USA at the time.

6. What this kind of testimony can offer us that written testimony cannot.

▶ **7.9 Conclusion**

Chapters 6 and 7 have aimed to introduce some of the main types of primary evidence that sports historians use, and to make them tangible by providing exercises. It may seem to be an overwhelming list; but it is important for you to get a sense of the potential resources that may be available to you. It should also be clear that many of these sources require specialised research skills that will require training and practice if you wish to develop them seriously. However, the vast amount of material covered here should have alerted you to possibilities, and helped you to develop the kind of research questions that you need to pose to get evidence from your sources.

8 Developing Your Own Sports History Project

We started this book by asking what sports history is. By this stage, you should have a clear idea of the different forms that this sub-discipline of history takes, along with an overview of the key themes in sports historiography, and a sense of what primary research can involve. In this final chapter, we are going to look at the ways in which you can apply this historical sensibility to your own work as a sports historian, using the focus of developing your own sports history project. This chapter is designed to help you create original and independent sports history writing that is scholarly and critical. It is about writing on sport in context, and not simply collecting events and facts and then narrating them. You should be aiming to produce work that is as professional as you can make it for its target audience, and that could make a genuine contribution to our knowledge of what sport was like in the past.

To achieve excellence in your writing, your project will need to stand out on a number of fronts. The basic requirements include accuracy and authority. No reader will be impressed with a project that contains factual errors (say, getting the year of a club's foundation wrong, or erroneously identifying an individual in your sport's history), or with one where the author does not seem to have any kind of expertise on the subject matter. Beyond that, the characteristics that impress in any historical writing are originality; a clearly defined set of research questions that are posed, explored, and answered; mastery of the secondary literature; a clear and appropriate methodology; an awareness of what the project contributes to the historiography; and a polished, professional writing style that addresses the readers at an appropriate level without patronising them or deferring to them. To help you towards this achievement, this chapter will explore the following themes: the project's remit; identifying a subject area; secondary reading; research questions; locating and using primary sources; and structuring and writing the project. To exemplify the processes covered, I have created a hypothetical project on the history of swimming, which will develop as we go through the chapter. This project's stages will appear in a box headed 'My project' at the end of each section, and will be written from the first-person perspective of a student. Please remember that this chapter does not stand alone: I have assumed that you will use it in conjunction with the rest of this book. You must also use it in conjunction with the relevant programme and module specifications from your own course: the guidance here is offered in general terms, and cannot be used to supersede any specific remit of any institution's programme.

▶ 8.1 The project's remit

Whatever the project, you are writing it for someone to read. If it is a dissertation towards a degree course, then your readers are your examiners, although you should also aspire to reach beyond them. Most degree courses require their students to produce a dissertation of some kind. This can go by various other names, including 'final year project' or 'independent project'. Whatever the name, the remit will be similar. The student has to produce a substantial piece of work, usually in the range of 6000–12,000 words at undergraduate level, and longer at taught postgraduate level. The point of the project will vary from course to course, and from institution to institution, and it is important to check the specific aims and learning outcomes of your degree's project before you start on it. There will also be variation between subjects – a physics dissertation, for example, will have a very different remit from a film studies one. However, the basic aim of all dissertations is to give you the opportunity to design and execute a discreet and defined piece of research. It is there to give you experience in identifying an issue that deserves to be researched, reading around the issue in the existing literature so that you can see what has been done and what remains to be done, asking research questions or setting hypotheses about the issue, devising a methodology that will get you the information you need, answering the question, and presenting the finished work in a professional way. If you can do this well at an undergraduate level, then you will have proved your ability as a researcher and developed a set of skills that you can use for postgraduate research, or for countless workplace and professional applications. This, then, is your audience: the examiners who will be impressed with what you have done, and will reward you accordingly.

In single subject degree courses, the remit for the dissertation will tend to be straightforward: the student will have to design and execute a piece of research within the degree's subject area (chemistry, education, archaeology, or whatever) and in line with the subject area's protocols and traditions. However, in multidisciplinary degree courses such as sports-based ones, and any others that include the word 'Studies', things can be a bit more complicated. Each of the parent subjects – history, sociology, physiology, psychology, business, and so on – will have its own protocols and traditions. Many courses have tended to develop fairly generic sports studies type protocols for dissertations, but these have tended to be overly scientific in approach, a development that can be problematic and confusing for the student who wishes to do a sports history dissertation, as it can often prescribe a particular structure that is not always suitable for historical writing. In particular, very few historians feel comfortable writing about their 'evidence' and their 'discussion' in separate sections, as is often a requirement in science-based subject. As sports history matures and grows in confidence, courses are developing more bespoke routes for the different subject areas. It is therefore important to work with your tutors in identifying an appropriate structure for your project.

My project 1

As a historian with an interest in sport, a desire to make the past of sport more widely known, and a wish to understand the roots of current issues and problems in sport, I have decided to do my project in sports history.

▶ ## 8.2 Identifying a subject area

By the time you come to make your choice about the subject of your project, you should be clear about the disciplinary area in which you wish to work. If you know that your academic strengths lie in physiology, for example, then there is no point in you developing a sociological topic. If you have strengths in social and cultural aspects of sport, and find sports history interesting, then you should consider this as your area. Similarly, if you are a history student with an interest in sport, then consider doing your dissertation in sports history. However, identifying your broad area of work is probably easier than picking a topic. For a start, history is – as should be clear by this stage in the book – not the kind of area where you can set up a controlled experiment in a laboratory, or where you can define and limit all of the variables in a predictable way.

A number of factors should influence your choice of topic. First, and perhaps most importantly, it must be something in which you are interested. There is no point in going for what you might see as an easy option if the subject matter does not engage you. Second, it is worth considering your existing knowledge of the area. If you have only a small proportion of time spread over a busy year in which to design, research, and write the project, then pre-knowledge is important. These remarks apply to any project: they are not restricted to sports history. In the specific area of sports history, you need to think about what is realistic and viable within your timeframe and resources. Factors that can influence viability are numerous, including:

Size Some topics are simply too big. No undergraduate, for example, could write a worthwhile narrative history of the Olympic Games as a dissertation with any originality. Similarly, some topics may be too small.

Language If you do not read the language or languages in which the primary sources were written, then you are at a disadvantage. Many sources that are relevant to sports history are available in English translation, such as Homer for the ancient Olympic Games or dubbed versions of Leni Riefenstahl's *Olympia*, but you are unlikely to find significant amounts of the kind of primary sources covered in Chapters 5, 6, and 7 – newspapers, diaries, official records – in anything other than their original language. This is not to say that you should not use translations if appropriate: but remember that however good the translations, they have gone through a mediation process that puts them at a remove from their original contexts.

Access to sources We have already seen that access to sources is not a neutral or universal activity, and you need to identify a topic area for which the primary sources exist and are freely accessible. There is no point, for example, in aiming to write a project on the early history of a local club if that club has not kept its records from that period.

Access to places If you are interested in a topic based on the history of a sporting place, or in which site visits are important, then plan within sensible budgets of time and expenses. A project on the remains of ancient Olympia will be great if you can visit the site and spend quality research time there, but will be of limited value if you get no closer than a virtual tour on the Internet.

Access to people If the opportunities of oral history covered in Chapter 7 interest you, then you need to work with who is available. Are there people still alive who can help? Can you get access to them?

Originality Although no two historians approach the same sources in the same way, it is important to look for a new topic in your own research. This is likely to involve applying large themes from the existing historiography on to a new case study, or approaching a familiar topic with a new theoretical perspective.

These are some of the areas you need to weigh up as potential limitations on your sports history dissertation. Use these pointers to help you identify a realistic topic on which you wish to work. Talk to your tutors about areas that could work, paying particular attention to the quantity and quality of the primary sources, and whether they can support the project. By the end of this process, you should be able to identify a broad area: say, lacrosse in the late nineteenth century, gymnastics in the 1960s, sport and diplomacy, the history of disability sport, or the heritage of sport.

My project 2

I have identified swimming in England in the nineteenth and twentieth centuries. This does not present me with any language problems, I will not have to spend too much time or money on travel for research, it appears to be manageable in size, and I already have a grounding in swimming from my own participation since childhood. I am also aware of some problematic issues in swimming, such as equality of access across some ethnic and religious lines, and of swimming's importance in contemporary debates about public health (particularly obesity), and am interested to know the roots of these issues.

▶ 8.3 Secondary reading

All dissertations require a significant amount of reading in the existing literature. In part, you should use this as a way of refining your dissertation's subject from the broad topic area to the specific. Reading what is already out there shows you what has been done, what can be done in an area, and what the gaps in the literature are. For example, if you are interested in the history of sport and diplomacy as your big topic area, reading the existing literature will show you the kind of case studies that have already been done, and may suggest new ones awaiting the sports historian. This reading is also essential for giving you an engagement with the historiographical issues covered in Chapters 3 and 4 as they apply to your area of research. Critical reading will allow you, for example, to identify any particular theories that have dominated the area. An excellent dissertation will always show this kind of engagement. Careful reading, particularly in the reference and bibliographical sections of the existing literature, will also give you an idea of the primary sources that exist. These may be specific, as when an author uses a particular newspaper or set of minutes that you think will be of value to you. Or they may be generic: seeing how a historian has used diaries, letters, photographs, or local newspapers could inspire you to look for such types of evidence in your topic area. This reading will help you to assess the best methodologies for your project: there is nothing like improving your own historical interviewing technique, for example, than a critical reflection on the quality of the interviews conducted by a published sports historian. Remember to keep full and accurate notes, and to give your reading some structure, as it is likely that you will need to write a critical commentary on the secondary sources as a literature review in the final project. Again, you should work with your tutor on what your institution requires here. You should be able to recognise who the key authors are and what the key texts have been, the timing of the literature, what the main issues in any debates within the area are, and how your own work could add to the literature. Moreover, your reading must encompass more than sport. Sports history is all about linking play to context, and you need to do some contextual reading if you hope to pull this off. So, for example, a project on women's sport that does not include any reading on women's non-sporting history will always be in a vacuum.

My project 3

From this process, I have identified that not much has been written on swimming in this period, and that a local case study could be a realistic project. This would allow me to take a number of themes from the national literature on sport and its social context – such as public health and hygiene, the growth of leisure time and disposable income, the breakdown of taboos about mixed sex sport, amateurism and voluntarism in sport, and the application of technology to sport – and apply them to a real place in a defined period of time. I have chosen the city of Southampton. This choice has been influenced by a number of factors. First, it is where I work, and so access to sources, locations, and people will be relatively easy. Second, I know from working there and swimming there something about the location and timing of the different swimming sites that it has had. I know from reading some of the city's local history that it had its share of public health concerns during the period that interests me, linked at different points to poor housing, disease, and unemployment, and that it has had, at various points, a local authority that has promoted sport, often in pioneering ways. I have seen from some of the literature on swimming the kinds of sources that I could expect to find, and feel that this project would add something to our knowledge of swimming, and our knowledge of an industrial and maritime city.

▶ 8.4 Research questions

Once you have defined the exact subject, you will still need a critical and analytical focus. Remember that the sports history dissertation is not simply a chance for you to tell a story about something in sport's past. The project needs to be driven by clearly defined questions, akin to hypotheses in a scientific project. The questions will, of course, vary from subject to subject – and, indeed, from student to student, as it should be clear by now that every historian brings an individual perspective to the subject, and no two students would approach the same material with identical questions. Your questions will evolve from your secondary reading. They need to encompass both the big picture and the detailed case study, and to act as drivers for the research. You should also make sure that they suit the kind of research skills you have. For example, if you know that you have strengths in interviewing people and analysing their responses, then questions that are based around people's perceptions and impressions of what sport was like and what it meant to them will be useful. If, on the other hand, you are good with statistical data, then questions based on quantification that will generate numerical answers will be appropriate. It is through these that you can further refine the focus of your work. As such, they must be open questions, capable of complex and flexible answers, rather than closed questions that can simply be answered in one word. Moreover, unlike the hypothesis approach in sports science, you are likely to find your questions changing during the course of the research as the evidence throws up new lines of enquiry, and you need to appreciate their fluid nature from the outset.

My project 4

1. What swimming facilities have the people of Southampton had in the period 1880–1980?

2. What have been the roles of public, private, voluntary, commercial, and educational agencies in the provision of these swimming facilities?

3. How did Southampton's swimmers use their facilities?

4. What was the interrelationship between swimming as a recreational activity and swimming as a serious sport in the period?

5. What evidence survives of any swimming sites that were closed down during the period?

These questions are designed to ensure that the project looks at swimming in its social, political, and economic contexts, while also keeping a focus on the specific circumstances of Southampton. Question 5 is designed to bring in a sports heritage angle. Overall, they play to my strength of an interest in the provision of sport and how people interacted with it, and how this changes over time.

▶ 8.5 Locating and using primary sources

Your secondary reading should have helped you to identify the types of primary sources you could use. You now need to be more specific, and locate the exact ones that will help you to answer your research questions. What these sources are will vary hugely from project to project. Some sample questions can help you to work out what you need to ask.

1. Was the subject of your interest covered by an organisation that kept records (such as a club, a governing body, a branch of central or local government)? If yes, then has that evidence survived? Where is it now?

2. Was the subject likely to have been covered in newspapers, magazines, or any other form of the media? Would this coverage have been in the national media, the local media, or both?

3. Are there likely to be people still alive who lived through the events you wish to research? Can you locate them?

4. Did your subject take place before or after the invention of photography and/or film? If such visual sources survive, where are they?

5. Are there any museums, halls of fame, or specialist archives dedicated to your sport?

There are many sources available that can help you locate the appropriate primary evidence. These include reference books on archive holdings, and online guides to archives, some of which are listed in the Bibliography section. The great value of online guides is the way in which they can lead you into the catalogues of national, regional, local, and specialised archives. The time and resource constraints that you are likely to face mean that the evidence needs to be physically accessible to you, which is one of the reasons why I advocate local studies of sports history at this level.

Once you have found the sources, what do you do with them? Many students get worked up about methodologies, regardless of the discipline in which they are working. The simple thing to keep in mind is that your methodology must be one that will help you answer your questions (or, in a science-based project, your hypotheses). As a sports historian, your methodology needs to be based around the appropriate primary sources, and needs to be designed to get the information out of those sources that will allow you to answer your questions. The starting point is the nature of the evidence, informed by anything – good or bad – that you have learnt from published historians' methods in the existing literature. The methodology needs to be realistic within your time and resource limits. You need to be clear early on in the primary research about what you are doing with it. Very little of originality can come from a method that is simply based on reading all the relevant documents and writing down what happened. Such an approach could give us a decent story, but it will never answer the kind of research questions you should be asking. Asking the following questions could help you devise the appropriate methodology for your project.

1. What are my research questions? (see above)

2. What is my primary evidence?

3. What methods have I learnt about from the relevant historiography, and from other research methodology books? What do I like or dislike about these methods? How relevant will they be for my project?

4. How am I going to sample my primary evidence? (For example, if it is based on newspapers, which papers will you use? If it is based on oral history, how will you choose your interviewees?)

5. What questions am I going to ask of that evidence? This is the key point here if you want to avoid storytelling. Asking the kind of questions of your primary evidence that we have explored in Chapters 5, 6, and 7 will ensure that you are critical and analytical from the start.

6. What kind of comparisons between different sources can I do? How can different sources complement and supplement each other?

7. How am I going to arrange and manage my notes? Is a qualitative coding approach useful?

8. What value could such accessories as timelines, maps, glossaries, and biographical notes of protagonists have?

Make sure that while carrying out your research, you have all of these factors in place. Analyse as you go: you will find that historical research lends itself to constant building, based on reflection and reassessment as you move through the sources, in a way that scientific research is not. You will also find yourself returning to the secondary reading at key points, to allow yourself to read out from the evidence (say, to find out the circulation figures of a newspaper, or to find out about the career of someone mentioned in a letter). Obviously, you must ensure that your notes are 100% accurate: any misquotation or error in transcription may cause you to misrepresent the evidence.

My project 5

I have identified local newspapers, local council minutes, and maps and photographs from throughout the period to find out where all of Southampton's swimming pools were, and when they were built and, if appropriate, closed down. Local newspapers will also identify the providers of each pool, such as the local council, a private company, or a school, and research into the archives of some sample providers will give me information about their respective roles. To get a sense of the interactions that went on around swimming – how people used their pools, the role of recreation and competition – I will conduct a series of interviews with people of various ages who used different pools. I will recruit the interviewees through advertisements in the local newspaper, record and transcribe semi-structured interviews, and analyse their responses using appropriate codings. I will also return to press coverage of major competitions, and to the record books of sample swimming clubs, to find out more about the competitive side. Finally, I will compare the old maps with a current map to find the locations of former pools, and explore the areas on foot, annotating the maps and taking photographs of any archaeological evidence.

▶ 8.6 Structuring the project

A sports history project can come in many forms, and you should work with your tutor to ensure that your own project makes sense both in relation to its disciplinary nature and to the requirements of any programme specifications. It is likely that if your course is rooted in sports science, then you may have to structure your work in a formal reporting way, with such sections as 'Rationale', 'Literature review', 'Methodology', Results', and 'Discussion'. Sports history can be written like this, but it is rather artificial: in particular, the idea of keeping 'results' and 'discussion' separate is difficult in a project based on primary evidence that you, the researcher, did not create. If your course can be flexible, then try to negotiate a structure that allows you to write your sports history dissertation in a format similar to a sports history journal article – or, indeed, to model it as a short book. The Introduction can set up the issue, review the existing literature, explain the methodology, and ask the research questions. You can think of this as a section that explains what the project is, why you are doing it, and how you are doing it. You can then use chapters to deliver the material. The exact structure will vary hugely from project to project, but a rough formula that moves from the big picture in Chapter 1 on to the specific case study in Chapters 2 and 3 is helpful. You should set up an appropriate relationship between your primary and secondary sources throughout, even in the case study chapters, to show that you are always keeping the bigger contexts in mind. Finally, you must write a solid Conclusion where you answer the research questions that were posed in the Introduction, and where you relate your project to the existing historiography to show what you have added.

My project 6

Introduction   The scope of the project; the reasons why it needs to be studied, including a critical review literature to show the gaps; the research questions; the methods and sources employed.

Chapter 1   Swimming in England, 1880–1980. This will be a predominantly secondary-based chapter which gives a brief narrative history of the subject and identifies the critical themes that have emerged from that history. These include the respective roles of the state and the private sector in providing sports facilities; the links between public health and the promotion of swimming; the interrelationship between recreational and elite swimming; and the links between swimming pool design, health and safety legislation, technology, and public taste.

Chapter 2   Swimming pools in Southampton. This chapter will concentrate on the pools and their providers, always linking back to the political and commercial context of each pool's lifespan. The evidence here would come from newspapers, local authority minutes and annual reports, historical maps, and historical photographs.

Chapter 3   Swimmers in Southampton. This chapter will explore the experience of swimming from the perspective of those who did it, combining recreational and competitive swimmers. It will also explore the meanings that people have attached to swimming pools that have been demolished. This evidence will be drawn mainly from original interviews.

Conclusion   This will answer the research questions set in the Introduction, and will make links to the existing historiography of swimming and of Southampton.

Appendix   I will include a gazetteer of all swimming pools built during the project's time period, with a map to identify the locations.

Bibliography and References   A full and comprehensive list of every item, primary and secondary, used in the project.

▶ 8.7 Conclusion

Carrying out your own original research in sports history is an exciting prospect, but it is important not to get carried away. By designing a realistic project for which primary sources exist, you can add to our historical knowledge. You know that you have made a difference when an examiner reads a project and learns something from it, so taking the time to think through the subject matter and research thoroughly is in everyone's interests. By taking an under-explored subject, or applying existing ideas to a new locality or different sport, you can approach this. Then, by thinking like a sports historian, and applying this book's lessons of critical thinking, historiography, and source analysis to your work, you can achieve it.

Conclusion

The main aim of this book has been to make sports history an accessible and attractive option. Whether you are studying sport as part of a multidisciplinary programme, studying history, or simply interested in sport's past, this book should have helped you to think critically and holistically about our approaches to the past. What conclusions can we draw from this exploration?

The first conclusion is that sports history, like any kind of history, is clearly far from easily recoverable. Much of our everyday engagement with sport is governed by notions of certainty: the ball was in or it was out, and athlete X ran faster than athlete Y. In addition, dominant scientific paradigms in sport – particularly those based in physiology and biomechanics – value unambiguous answers. However, any consideration of sports history will show that there are far too many variables at work to make such certainty achievable in this discipline. The primary evidence that we have to work with is always inherently subjective, partial, fragmented, and incomplete. Even when we read around it, and attempt to triangulate or corroborate different sources, we remain in the hands of generations of annalists, journalists, politicians, administrators, archivists, and others who created the evidence in the first place, or filed it and protected it for the present. The many hands involved, and the different needs and organisational agendas of all those levels, make it impossible to simply see what happened in the past. We cannot simply experience an old football match or horse race as if we were there. Instead, we have to approach it through the layers and filters created by its original recorders and the people who have maintained the record. This is not to say that there is no such thing as historical truth: things undoubtedly happened in the past, and some of those things left evidence behind. However, it is important to remember when approaching the evidence that it is not an objective record, and you need to develop skills to deal with it accordingly, as discussed in Chapters 5, 6, and 7. With these skills in place, you can move beyond the hope of finding a simple narrative in the past of sport, and work more realistically – and in a more stimulating way – on the nuances and multiple interpretations that make up historical research.

Our second conclusion, based on the discussions in Chapters 3 and 4, is that the historian plays an important role in the creation of history. This is now a truism of historical study, but one that should not be underestimated. Sports historians come to the subject with all kinds of affiliations, assumptions, theories, and preferences. Some of them are explicit about their theories, while others are not. Some are, in Booth's phrase, 'reflexive' about their relationship with the past, while others try to remain detached.[1] Some historians make a point of asking present-centred questions of their subject matter, while others prefer to work purely from the evidence. Some work at micro-levels, others at macro-levels. Apart from the diversity of approaches, historians write their sports history up in different ways: in narratives or synthesis, by theme or by chronology, in books or on websites, for academics or for fans. As with the challenges involved in researching from the primary evidence, the point here is that there is no single way of doing history: it is necessarily a multifaceted and heterogeneous discipline. This book's analysis, and its activities and exercises, should have alerted you to this variety, and helped you develop a critical framework for dealing with sports historiography.

Linked to this conclusion is our third one, which is to note the ever-changing face of sports history as a discipline. The starting point here is to reflect on this book: twenty years ago, it would never have been written; whereas now, with a thriving sports history scene and a major investment in the subject from schools, universities, and publishers, it is viable. Chapter 3 explored the development of sport as a legitimate area for historians to study, but we cannot simply let the story finish there. You need to remain aware of the constant fluctuations in what gets covered by sports historians if you are to engage with the discipline. Keep an eye, for example, on the ways in which sports history engages with other academic disciplines: not just sociology and physical education, as discussed in Chapter 3, but also cultural studies, geography, archaeology, and heritage studies.[2] Look at the ways in which increasingly diverse minority groups get embraced by sports historians as the history from below agenda evolves in a post-colonial, multicultural, and equal opportunities setting. The past three decades have seen gender and ethnicity added to class as a category: now look for religious groups, people with different disabilities, and increasingly diverse national, ethnic, and migrant groups to appear in sports history.[3] Get involved with the ongoing debate within sports history about post-modernism as a theoretical perspective, a debate made accessible by Murray Phillips' recent collection of essays.[4] This is not always an easy area to penetrate. As Douglas Booth stresses, 'sports historians have generally shied away from postmodernism',[5] with its emphasis on the subjectivity or historical knowledge, the relativity of all sources, and the impossibility of historical truth. This debate is bigger than sports history: it is going on throughout the discipline of history as a whole, sometimes with potentially dangerous implications when applied to events such as the Holocaust.[6] However, a 'critical' and 'cautious'[7] engagement with post-modernism can sharpen our approaches, as it gets us asking awkward questions about such areas as the role of language in constructing history, the silences in the evidence, and the political assumptions about power, gender, class, and ethnicity behind the standard narrative of how sport developed over time. These are just some of the ways in which you can use this book as the foundation for your engagement with sports history, and add to it as you study both old and new historiography, and conduct your own research.

A final conclusion is that sports history is not simply a dead subject ready for academic discussion. All cultural activities have their own sense of the past, embodied in their traditions and customs, and in the ways in which things from the past are remembered or forgotten. Think beyond sport for a moment, to such phenomena as the historical overtones of the last night of the Proms, the celebration of the past in the Rock and Roll Hall of Fame, or the emphasis on certain long-dead authors' works in many countries' dramatic traditions: Shakespeare in England, Ibsen in Norway, or Goethe in Germany. All sporting cultures have their own versions of this infatuation with the past, seen in the many forms we explored in Chapter 2. Museums, street names, statues, stadium names, replica kits, and the maintenance of customs past their cultural sell-by date are all examples of this trend. Working as a sports historian means having to recognise this culture, and you need to be prepared to interrogate it rather than simply accept it. This can be challenging, particularly if you are emotionally or institutionally committed to maintained mythologies, or if you have never asked awkward questions about why certain events or people get remembered while others get forgotten. Sports history is about live debates that affect the way we live now, seen most obviously in the demolition of old sports sites, the erection of memorial plaques, and the induction of certain people into halls of fame. Practising the kind of sports history advocated in this book – one that is critical, challenging, and provocative – can help you get involved with those debates in a sophisticated way.

Sports history is not easy. Doing it well entails empathy, imagination, and numerous critical skills, and it requires you to think and write theoretically and practically. It can also be frustrating, as the impossibility of recovering the past in anything other than a fragmented and partial way hits you. However, it is worth the effort. Being able to interrogate the past can add perspective to your understanding of sport in the present. It can help you to understand the similarities and differences that exist between sports cultures in different places, and it can enable you to compare and contrast across time and space. Knowing about the past helps you make sense of the present, and it can help you to understand change in sport that takes place in your own lifetime. By engaging with this book's themes, and by developing your historical skills through its activities, you should be able to set a solid foundation for your own work as a sports historian.

Glossary

This Glossary provides explanations of some of the more specialised words and phrases as they are used in the book. You should not use it as a dictionary; instead, use these explanations as a quick reference guide during your reading, and as the springboard for further thinking about sports history.

▶ Anachronism

Placing something in the wrong historical period. For example, it would be anachronistic to claim that 'Germany' won the 1990 football World Cup, as Germany was still divided into two nations and two football teams at the time, and the winners represented the Federal Republic (or West Germany). Although pointing such things out can lead to charges of pedantry, avoiding anachronisms is a basic skill for any historian.

▶ Archive

A collection of historical resources. Archives include those that house state-generated materials (such as those of central and local government, the military, and the law), as well as documents from religious, commercial, and voluntary agencies, and private family papers.

▶ Artefact

An object that was used by people in the past, and which historians can use to find out about the past. Artefacts for sports historians include old bats, balls, clothing, and other items used for sport.

▶ Chronology

A list of events arranged in the order that they happened. Many sports history texts include chronologies, or timelines, to show the sequence of events. Chronologies are crucial, both to give you the story and to help you avoid anachronism, but they should not be seen as the end aim of sports history.

► Common sense

The things you know without having to think. In academic discourse, this term is used to identify those things that we – as individuals and as members of communities and cultures – take for granted, and the things that we find challenged when something new or alternative is suggested. Historical research should always aim to challenge common sense assumptions, as it can help us to see the cultural roots of many things that we often accept as natural. The field of gender provides many good examples for sports historians. 'Common sense' may tell you that football is a male game, but historical research shows up plenty of female versions in many societies.

► Context

The setting in which something happens, and the ways in which features of that setting – geographical, economic, social, or cultural, for example – influence the aspect of history that you are studying.

► Cultural studies

Academic discipline dedicated to the selective study of culture and cultures. It usually encompasses literature, film, and media studies.

► Discipline

A field of academic study. For this book, the key disciplines are history and sports studies.

► Empathy

The ability to recognise the feelings and perceptions of others. For historians, empathy is important if we are to attempt to understand the choices and behaviour of people in past societies. It requires you to try to think beyond your own common sense worldview, and think about how you might feel about other situations.

▶ Ethnicity

The cultural aspects of identity based on a person's racial, national, religious, and cultural sense of self. It is more subtle and sophisticated a term than 'race', which tends to look only at biological differences between people. Ethnicity is now a central theme in historical research, including that conducted in sports history.

▶ Eurocentric

Holding a view of the world that is unconsciously governed by a purely European perspective. For example, a Eurocentric view of world football would not question the disproportionate number of places given to European teams in FIFA's World Cup competition. Much sport has been structured around unexamined Eurocentric views, and much sports history has been written from similar perspectives.

▶ Feminism

An ideology which emphasises the need for women to be given equality of opportunity with men in all areas of life. Many historians – including sports historians – have approached their subject matter from feminist perspectives, which tend to concentrate on gender relations and identity in past societies.

▶ Gender

Where sex is the biological difference between females and males, gender is the cultural identity that people have arising from these differences. To be 'male' or 'female' is a matter of sex; to be a 'man', a 'woman', a 'gentleman' or a 'lady' are matters of gender. As with ethnicity, gender is a central theme in historical research.

▶ Historiography

The representation of history, as opposed to the events of the past themselves, and the study of that representation and its methods.

▶ Ideology

A world view, influenced by political, economic, and cultural factors.

▶ Interdisciplinary

An academic approach that is informed by approaches and methods from two or more academic disciplines.

▶ Journal

An academic periodical that appears at regular intervals throughout the year. Its main audience is students and other academics, and its main market is in university and college libraries.

▶ Manuscript

Strictly a handwritten document (from Latin 'manus' [hand] and 'scribere' [to write]), this is one of the types of primary document that a historian will study. The term is often used more generally, though less accurately, for any historical document.

▶ Marxism

Political ideology based on the writings of Karl Marx, characterised by a critique of social stratification. In academic terms, it is a theoretical perspective that has influenced various disciplines, including history, with its emphasis on the role of class.

▶ Monograph

An academic book based heavily on primary, unpublished sources.

▶ Museum

Institution designed to collect, display, and interpret artefacts on a particular theme.

▶ Narrative

A story-based version of history, one that tends to concentrate on events rather than on analysis and interpretation.

▶ Oral history

Historical method based on the historian conducting original interviews with people who have lived through the events being researched.

▶ Polemic

A piece of writing that takes an argumentative and controversial point of view on an issue.

▶ Positivism

A philosophical approach to a subject that is based on scientific observation, and that assumes the researcher can be objective and impartial. In historiography, the label is applied to authors who attempt to approach the past without any acknowledgement of how their own position in time, and their autobiography, can affect their research.

▶ Post-modernism

A notoriously difficult term to define, post-modernism is a cultural trend rather than a specific theory, linked to a range of movements and events that have influenced politics and culture since the early twentieth century. In historiography, post-modernism is a collection of viewpoints which challenge many features of historical research, such as the nature of sources, the language of debate, the importance of particular events, and the possibility of historical reconstruction.

▶ Primary source

A piece of evidence that was created at the time the historian is studying.

▶ Reductionism

An analysis that concentrates on only one aspect of the historical society being studied, ignoring other features. Reductionist history is often linked to particular theoretical perspectives: for example, early Marxist historians were criticised for focusing on class while ignoring other aspects of past societies, such as gender and ethnicity.

▶ Relativism

A philosophical approach to a subject that recognises the links between the issue being studied and the person carrying out the study. It assumes that the researcher cannot be objective. In historiography, the label is applied to authors who acknowledge the influence that their autobiography and context can have on their research.

▶ Secondary source

A piece of evidence that was created after the time the historian is studying.

▶ Sociology

The academic study of societies.

▶ Sports science

Umbrella term for the academic study of sport from a scientific perspective. Exact content will vary from university to university, but physiology, psychology, biomechanics, and other aspects of the science of performance will figure highly.

▶ Sports studies

Umbrella term for the academic study of sport from a multifaceted perspective, usually combining some scientific disciplines (such as physiology and psychology) with some non-scientific ones (such as sociology, history, anthropology, media studies, and business studies).

▶ Synthesis (book)

A history book that brings together original research from many other authors and synthesises it into an accessible text.

▶ Text book

Book designed to complement a specific course of study; one that is tied to the course through its structure and content.

Notes

▶ Introduction

1. C. Gratton and I. Jones, *Research Methods for Sport Studies* (London: Routledge, 2004); D. Andrews, D. Mason and M. Silk, eds, *Qualitative Methods in Sports Studies* (Oxford: Berg, 2005); J. Thomas, J. Nelson and S. Silverman, *Research Methods in Physical Activity*, 5th edn (Champaign, IL: Human Kinetics, 2005).
2. M. Ntoumanis, *A Step-by-Step Guide to SPSS for Sport and Exercise Studies* (London: Routledge, 2001); G. Clarke and B. Humberstone, *Researching Women and Sport* (London: Macmillan, 1997).
3. See, for example, A. Veal, *Research Methods for Leisure and Tourism: A Practical Guide*, 2nd edn (Harlow: Prentice Hall, 1997); M. Clarke, M. Riley, E. Wilkie and R. Wood, *Researching and Writing Dissertations in Hospitality and Tourism* (London: Thomson Business Press, 1998).
4. Quality Assurance Agency for Higher Education, 'Subject Benchmark Statements, Hospitality, Leisure, Sport and Tourism' (2000), available at http://www.qaa.ac.uk/academicinfrastructure/benchmark/honours/hospitality.asp.
5. F. Galligan, C. Maskery, J. Spence, D. Howe, T. Barry, A. Ruston, and D. Crawford, *Advanced PE for Edexcel* (Oxford: Heinemann, 2000).
6. Gratton and Jones, op. cit, p. xii.
7. D. Booth, *The Field: Truth and Fiction in Sport History* (Abingdon: Routledge, 2005); N. Struna, 'Historical Research in Physical Activity', in Thomas, Nelson and Silverman, op. cit., pp. 215–30; D. Wiggins and D. Mason, 'The Socio-Historical Process in Sports Studies', in Andrews, Mason and Silk, eds, op. cit., pp. 39–64.
8. E.H. Carr, *What is History?* 2nd edn (London: Penguin, 2001); G. Elton, *The Practice of History* (Sydney: Sydney University Press, 1967); A. Marwick, *The New Nature of History: Knowledge, Evidence, Language* (Basingstoke: Palgrave, 2001); K. Jenkins, *Re-thinking History* (London: Routledge, 1991); J. Black and D.M. MacRaild, *Studying History*, 2nd edn (Basingstoke: Palgrave, 2000).

▶ Warm-up exercises

1. R. Askwith, *Feet in the Clouds: A Tale of Fell-Running and Obsession* (London: Aurum Press, 2004), pp. 206–10.
2. F. Bruno, *Eye of the Tiger: My Life* (London: Weidenfeld and Nicolson, 1992), p. 33.
3. Quoted in BBC, 'Football Legend George Best Dies', BBC News, 25 November 2005. Available at http://news.bbc.co.uk/1/hi/uk/4380332.stm, accessed 25 November 2005.
4. B. Morgan, 'South African Rugby', *South Africa: Alive with Possibility*, http://www.southafrica.info/ess_info/sa_glance/sports/rugby.htm, no date, accessed September 2005.
5. J. Myerson, *Not a Games Person* (London: Yellow Jersey Press, 2005), p. 99.
6. J.K. Rowling, *Harry Potter and the Philosopher's Stone* (London: Bloomsbury, 1997); J.K. Rowling (writing as Kennilworthy Whisp), *Quidditch Through the Ages* (London: Bloomsbury, 2001).
7. R. Harris, 'Empathy and History Teaching: An Unresolved Dilemma?', *Prospero*, 9 (1), 2003, pp. 31–8.
8. See D. Brailsford, *Sport, Time, and Society: The British at Play* (London: Routledge, 1991), pp. 53–6 for some examples of this.

▶ 1 What is sports history?

1. B. Southgate, *History: What and Why? Ancient, Modern, and Postmodern Perspectives* (London: Routledge, 1996), p. 1.
2. J. Black and D. MacRaild, *Studying History*, 2nd edn (Basingstoke: Palgrave, 2000), p. 4.
3. E.H. Carr, *What is History*? 2nd edn (London: Penguin, 2001); G. Elton, *The Practice of History* (Sydney: Sydney University Press, 1967); A. Marwick, *The New Nature of History: Knowledge, Evidence, Language* (Basingstoke: Palgrave, 2001); J. Tosh, *The Pursuit of History: Aims, Methods and New Directions in the Study of Modern History*, 3rd edn (London: Longman, 1999); Black and MacRaild, op. cit.
4. R.G. Collingwood, *The Idea of History* (Oxford: Oxford University Press, 1946), p. 9.
5. Carr, op. cit., p. 30.
6. Elton, op. cit., p. 71.
7. G. Connell-Smith and H.A. Lloyd, *The Relevance of History* (London: Heinemann, 1972), p. 41.

8. R. Holt, *Sport and the British: A Modern History* (Oxford: Oxford University Press, 1989), p. 2.
9. D. Booth, *The Field: Truth and Fiction in Sport History* (Abingdon: Routledge, 2005), p. 9.
10. W.G. Hoskins, *Local History in England*, 3rd edn (London: Longman, 1984), p. 30.
11. J.A. Mangan, 'Series Editor's Foreword', in N. Fishwick, ed., *English Football and Society, 1910–1950* (Manchester: Manchester University Press, 1989), p. vi.
12. Booth, op. cit., pp. 10–13.

▶ 2 The presence of the past in contemporary sport

1. Coca-Cola, 'Coca-Cola and the Olympic Movement', http://torchrelay. coca-cola.com/partnership.html, accessed October 2005.
2. Quorn Hunt, 'About Us', http://www.quornhunt.co.uk/pages.about. php3, accessed October 2005.
3. M. Gough, 'English Cricket's Finest Summer', 22 September 2005, http://www.bbc.co.uk/sport1/hi/cricket/aches_2005, accessed October 2005.
4. BBC, 'Brentford 0-0 Hartlepool', 29 January 2005, http://news.bbc. co.uk/sport1/hi/football/fa_cup/4197631.stm, accessed February 2005.
5. National Baseball Hall of Fame, 'Hall of Famer Lists', http://www. baseballhalloffame.org/hofers_and_honorees/lists/inducted.htm, accessed October 2005.
6. A. Wheewall, 'Haxey Hood: 700 Years of Tradition', http://www.wheewall.com/hood/, accessed January 2006. For an academic introduction to the Haxey Hood, see C. Parratt, 'Wasn't it Ironic? The Haxey Hood and the Great War', in M. Phillips, ed., *Deconstructing Sport History: A Postmodern Analysis* (Albany: State University of New York Press, 2006), pp. 131–46; C. Parratt, 'Of Place and Men, and Women: Topophilia and Gender in the Haxey Hood', *Journal of Sport History*, 27, 2000, pp. 229–45.
7. J. Arlott, *The Oxford Companion to Sports and Games* (Oxford: Oxford University Press, 1975), pp. 109–10.
8. For a wide-ranging introduction to this theme, see A. Beard, *The Language of Sport* (London: Routledge, 1998).
9. Ibid., pp. 19–21.
10. A. Guttmann (1978). *From Ritual to Record: The Nature of Modern Sports* (New York: Columbia University Press, 1978), p. 55.

11. N. Struna, 'Reframing the Direction of Change in the History of Sport', *International Journal of the History of Sport*, 18 (4), 2001, p. 5.

12. D. Young, *The Modern Olympic Games: A Struggle for Revival* (Baltimore: Johns Hopkins University Press, 1996).

13. Arlott, op. cit., pp. 67–8.

14. P. Young, *A History of British Football* (London: Stanley Paul, 1968), p. 3.

15. E. Dunning, J. Maguire, and R. Pearton, eds, 'Introduction: Sports in Comparative and Developmental Perspective', in *The Sports Process: A Comparative and Developmental Approach* (Champaign, IL: Human Kinetics, 1993), p. 1.

16. J. Rice, *Start of Play: The Curious Origins of Our Favourite Sports* (London: Prion, 1998), pp. 131–40.

17. C. Thomas, *The History of the British Lions* (Edinburgh: Mainstream, 1996), p. 13.

18. 'The Origins of the National Baseball Hall of Fame and Museum', http://www.baseballhalloffame.org/about/history.htm, accessed October 2005.

19. E. Hobsbawm and T. Ranger, eds, *The Invention of Tradition* (Cambridge: Cambridge University Press, 1992).

20. *The Book of the Club of True Highlanders* of 1881, quoted in H. MacLennan, 'Shinty's Place and Space in the World', *The Sports Historian*, 18 (1), 1998, p. 4.

21. F.A.M. Webster, *The Evolution of the Olympic Games, 1829 BC–1914 AD* (London: Heath Cranton & Oursely, 1914).

22. J. Tosh, *The Pursuit of History: Aims, Methods and New Directions in the Study of Modern History*, 3rd edn (London: Longman 1999), p. 177.

23. B. Whimpress, 'The Value of Facts in Sports History', *Sporting Traditions*, 9 (1), 1992, p. 12.

24. For a comprehensive listing of sports museums and halls of fame, with contact details and links, see 'Directory of Sports Museums', British Society of Sports History, http://www2.umist.ac.uk/sport/SPORTS%20HISTORY/index2b.html.

25. W. Vamplew, 'Museums and Halls of Fame', in R. Cox, G. Jarvie, and W. Vamplew, eds, *Encyclopedia of British Sport* (Oxford: ABC-Clio, 2000), p. 261.

26. R. Hewison, *The Heritage Industry: Britain in a Climate of Decline* (London: Methuen, 1987), p. 9.

27. English Heritage, *A Sporting Chance: Extra Time for England's Historic Sports Venues* (London: English Heritage, 2002); J. Wood, 'From Ashes to Dust: Who Cares about Sports Heritage?', *British Archaeology*, 85, 2005, http://www.britarch.ac.uk/ba/ba85/feat1.shtml, accessed December 2005.

28. AAP Architecture, 'Portfolio', http://www.aap-arc.co.uk/pf_dell.html, accessed October 2005.

29. Played in Britain, http://www.playedinbritain.co.uk/index.html, accessed December 2005.

▶ 3 Sport and historiography

1. R. Richardson, *The Debate on the English Revolution*, 3rd edn (Manchester: Manchester University Press, 1998); M. Marrus, *The Holocaust in History* (London: Pelican, 1987).

2. D. Nathan, *Saying It's So: A Cultural History of the Black Sox Scandal* (Urbana and Chicago: University of Illinois Press, 2003).

3. For an accessible overview of the main trends in history writing from the classical world to the twenty-first century, see A. Marwick, *The New Nature of History: Knowledge, Evidence, Language* (Basingstoke: Palgrave, 2001), pp. 51–151.

4. R. Evans, *Death in Hamburg: Society and Politics in the Cholera Years 1830–1910* (London: Penguin, 1990), p. vii.

5. W. Baker, 'The State of British Sport History', *Journal of Sport History*, 10 (1), 1983, 53–66; R. Holt, 'Sport and History: The State of the Subject in Britain', *Twentieth Century British History*, 7 (2), 1996, pp. 231–52; J. Lowerson, 'Opiate of the People and Stimulant of the Historian? — Some Issues in Sports History', in W. Lamont, ed., *Historical Controversies and Historians* (London: UCL Press, 1998), pp. 201–14; J. Hill, 'British Sports History: A Post-Modern Future?', *Journal of Sport History*, 23 (1), 1996, pp. 1–19; W. Vamplew, 'History', in R. Cox, G. Jarvie, and W. Vamplew, eds, *Encyclopedia of British Sport* (Oxford: ABC-Clio, 2000), pp. 178–80; M. Polley, 'History and Sport', in B. Houlihan, ed., *Sport and Society: A Student Introduction* (London: SAGE, 2003), pp. 49–64; M. Johnes, 'Resource Guide in Sports History', *LTSN Hospitality, Leisure, Sport and Tourism*, February 2003, http://www.hlst.heacademy.ac.uk/resources/sports_history.html, accessed May 2003.

6. D. Adair, 'Location, Location! Sports History and Academic Real Estate', *ASSH Bulletin*, 36, August 2002, pp. 11–14; D. Adair, 'Sports History in the "Antipodes" and "Australasia"', *Sporting Traditions*, 19 (1), 2002, pp. 65–74; R. Cashman, 'The Making of Sporting Traditions', *Bulletin* [of the Australian Society for Sports History], 1989, pp. 15–28; B. Whimpress, 'The Value of Facts in Sports History', *Sporting Traditions*, 9 (1), 1992, pp. 2–15.

7. N. Struna, 'Sport History', in J. Massengale and R. Swanson, eds, *The History of Exercise and Sport Science* (Champaign, IL: Human Kinetics,

1997), pp. 143–79; S. Pope, *The New American Sport History: Recent Approaches and Perspectives* (Champaign, IL: University of Illinois Press, 1997); S. Riess, 'The Historiography of American Sport', *Organization of American Historians Magazine of History*, 7, 1992, available at http://www.oah.org/pubs/magazine/sport/riess.html, accessed July 2005.

8. A. Krüger, 'Puzzle Solving: German Sport Historiography of the Eighties', *Journal of Sport History*, 17 (2), 1990, pp. 261–77.

9. J. Arbena, 'History of Latin American Sports: The End Before the Beginning?', *Sporting Traditions*, 16 (1), 1999, pp. 23–31.

10. Richard Cox manages the British Society of Sports History's online Bibliographic Service, which contains the 'Annual Bibliographies of Publications on the History of Sport in the English Language', 'Bibliography of Publications on the History of British Sport (to 2000)', and the 'Select Bibliography of Contemporary (Primary) Publications on British Sport 1800 to 1920'. In addition, see R. Cox, *Sport in Britain: A Bibliography of Historical Publications 1800–1988* (Manchester: Manchester University Press, 1991); R. Cox, *History of Sport: A Guide to the Literature and Sources of Information* (Frodsham: Sports History Publishing, 1994); R. Cox, *British Sport: A Bibliography to 2000* in Three Volumes: Volume 1, *Nationwide Histories* (London: Frank Cass, 2003), Volume 2, *Local Histories* (London: Frank Cass, 2003), Volume 3, *Biographical Studies of British Sportsmen, Sportswomen and Animals* (London: Frank Cass, 2003).

11. P. Egan, *Boxiana: Or Sketches of Ancient and Modern Pugilism* (London: G. Smeeton, 1812); P. Warner, *The Book of Cricket*, 4th edn (London: Sporting Handbooks, 1945); T.A. Cook, *A History of the English Turf* (London: Virtue, 1905). See Cox, op. cit. (1991) for a comprehensive listing of the academic and popular historiography of most sports and localities.

12. D. Kyle, 'E. Norman Gardiner: Historian of Ancient Sport', *International Journal of the History of Sport*, 8 (1), 1991, pp. 28–55.

13. Lowerson, op. cit. (1998), p. 201.

14. See, for example, Marwick, op. cit. (2001), pp. 88–151.

15. For a brief overview of *Annales* and guidance to further reading, see ibid., pp. 90–96.

16. E.P. Thompson, *The Making of the English Working Class*, revised edn (Harmondsworth: Pelican, 1980), p. 12.

17. Lowerson, op. cit. (1998), p. 202.

18. D. Brailsford, *Sport and Society: Elizabeth to Anne* (London: Routledge and Kegan Paul, 1969); J.A. Mangan, *Athleticism in the Victorian and Edwardian Public School: The Emergence and Consolidation of an Educational Ideology* (Cambridge: Cambridge University Press,

1981); T. Mason, *Association Football and English Society, 1863–1915* (Hassocks: Harvester Press, 1980).

19. F. Leonard, *A Guide to the History of Physical Education*, 3rd edn (Westport, CT: Greenwood Press, 1947); P. McIntosh, *Physical Education in England since 1800*, 2nd edn (London: Bell, 1968).

20. K. Watson, *The Crossing* (London: Headline, 2000), pp. 122–31.

21. E. Dunning and K. Sheard, *Barbarians, Gentlemen and Players: A Sociological Study of the Development of Rugby Football* (Oxford: Martin Robertson, 1979).

22. E. Dunning, P. Murphy, and J. Williams, *The Roots of Football Hooliganism: An Historical and Sociological Study* (London: Routledge & Kegan Paul, 1988).

23. J. Horne, A. Tomlinson, and G. Whannel, *Understanding Sport: An Introduction to the Sociological and Cultural Analysis of Sport* (London: Spon, 1999), p. 73.

24. T. Collins, 'History, Theory and the "Civilizing Process"', *Sport in History*, 25 (2), 2005, pp. 289–306.

25. J. MacAloon, *This Great Symbol: Pierre de Coubertin and the Origins of the Modern Olympic Games* (Chicago: University of Chicago Press, 1981), pp. xi–xii.

26. T. Collins, *Rugby's Great Split: Class, Culture and the Origins of Rugby League Football* (London: Frank Cass, 1998), p. xi.

27. D. Booth, *The Field: Truth and Fiction in Sport History* (Abingdon: Routledge, 2005), p. 211.

28. A. Harvey, *Football: The First Hundred Years: The Untold Story* (London: Routledge, 2005), p. xxiii.

29. R. Guha, *A Corner of a Foreign Field: The Indian History of a British Sport* (London: Picador, 2002), p. xv.

30. K. Robbins, *The Eclipse of a Great Power: Modern Britain, 1870–1975* (Harlow: Longman, 1983), pp. 157–9; K. Morgan, *The People's Peace: British History 1945–1989* (Oxford: Oxford University Press, 1990), pp. 257–8.

31. *Contemporary British History*, 14 (2), 2000, 'Amateurs and Professionals in Post-War British Sport'.

32. R. Holt, *Sport and the British: A Modern History* (Oxford: Oxford University Press, 1989); S. Simon, *Jackie Robinson and the Integration of Baseball* (Hoboken, NJ: Wiley, 2002); D. McComb, *Sports in World History* (London: Routledge, 2004).

33. W. Fotheringham, *Roule Britannia: A History of Britons in the Tour de France* (London: Yellow Jersey Press, 2005); E. Asinof, *Eight Men Out: The Black Sox and the 1919 World Series* (New York: Owl Books, 2000); S. Reeve, *One Day in September* (London: Faber and Faber, 2000).

34. S. Rae, *W.G. Grace: A Life* (London: Faber & Faber, 1998); D. Remnick, *King of the World* (London: Picador, 1999).
35. See, for example, N. Hornby, *Fever Pitch: A Fan's Life* (London: Victor Gollancz, 1992); L. Thompson, *The Dogs: A Personal History of Greyhound Racing* (London: Chatto & Windus, 1994); C. Sprawson, *The Haunts of the Black Masseuer: The Swimmer As Hero* (London: Jonathan Cape, 1992); T. Ecott, *Neutral Buoyancy: Adventures in a Liquid World* (London: Penguin, 2002).
36. RL1908, http://www.rl1908.com; Baseball Almanac, http://www.baseball-almanac.com; soccerbase, http://www.soccerbase.com. All accessed October 2005.
37. See, for example, 'large-scale thematic coverage of class' in R. Gruneau, *Class, Sports, and Social Development* (Amherst, MA: University of Massachusetts Press, 1983); J. Hargreaves, *Sport, Power and Culture: A Social and Historical Analysis of Popular Sports in Britain* (Cambridge: Polity, 1986); M. Polley, *Moving the Goalposts: A History of Sport and Society since 1945* (London: Routledge, 1998), pp. 111–34. For case studies, see, for example, S. Jones, *Sport, Politics and the Working Class: Organised Labour and Sport in Inter-War Britain* (Manchester: Manchester University Press, 1988); R. Holt, ed., *Sport and the Working Class in Modern Britain* (Manchester: Manchester University Press, 1990); G. Gems, *Windy City Wars: Labor, Leisure, and Sport in the Making of Chicago* (Lanham, Maryland: Scarecrow Press, 1997); R. Rosenzweig, *Eight Hours for What We Will: Workers and Leisure in an Industrial City, 1870–1920* (Cambridge: Cambridge University Press, 1983); J. Lowerson, *Sport and the English Middle Classes, 1870–1914* (Manchester: Manchester University Press, 1993); P. Bailey, *Leisure and Class in Victorian England: Rational Recreation and the Contest for Control* (London: Routledge & Kegan Paul, 1978).
38. For an introduction to Gramsci's influence on the analysis of sport, see D. Rowe, 'Antonio Gramsci: Sport, Hegemony and the National-Popular', in R. Giulianotti, ed., *Sport and Modern Social Theorists* (Basingstoke: Palgrave, 2004), pp. 97–110.
39. S. Jones, *Workers at Play: A Social and Economic History of Leisure 1918–1939* (London: Routledge & Kegan Paul, 1986); S. Jones, *Sport, Politics and the Working Class: Organised Labour and Sport in Inter-War Britain* (Manchester: Manchester University Press, 1988).
40. John Hargreaves, *Sport, Power and Culture: A Social and Historical Analysis of Popular Sports in Britain* (Cambridge: Polity, 1986), p. 1.
41. As with social class, the historiography of gender in sport is huge. For large-scale coverage, see S. Cahn, *Coming On Strong: Gender and Sexuality in Twentieth-Century Women's Sport* (New York: The Free Press, 1994); A. Guttmann, *Women's Sport: A History* (New York: Columbia

University Press, 1991); J. Hargreaves, *Sporting Females: Critical Issues in the History and Sociology of Women's Sports* (London: Routledge, 1994). Case studies include J.A. Mangan and R. Park, eds, *From 'Fair Sex' to Feminism: Sport and the Socialisation of Women in the Industrial and Post-Industrial Eras* (London: Frank Cass, 1987); P. Vertinsky, *The Eternally Wounded Woman: Women, Exercise, and Doctors in the Late Nineteenth Century* (Manchester: Manchester University Press, 1990); P. McDevitt, *May the Best Man Win: Sport, Masculinity and Nationalism in Great Britain and the Empire, 1880–1935* (Basingstoke: Palgrave, 2004). For a critical review of gender as a factor in the sports history establishment, see P. Vertinsky, 'Time Gentlemen Please: The Space and Place of Gender in Sport History', in M. Phillips, ed., *Deconstructing Sport History: A Postmodern Analysis* (Albany: State University of New York Press, 2006), pp. 227–44.

42. See, for example, J. Sammons, 'Race and Sport: A Critical, Historical Explanation', *Journal of Sport History*, 21 (3), 1994, pp. 203–77; E. Cashmore, *Black Sportsmen* (London: Routledge, 1982); Polley, op. cit. (1998), pp. 135–59; G. Jarvie, ed., *Sport, Racism and Ethnicity* (Brighton: Falmer Press, 1985); P. Levine, *Ellis Island to Ebbetts Field: Sport and the American Jewish Experience* (Oxford: Oxford University Press, 1992); A. Bass, *Not the Triumph but the Struggle: the 1968 Olympics and the Making of the Black Athlete* (Minneapolis: University of Minnesota Press, 2002); J. Bloom, *To Show What an Indian can Do: Sports at Native American Boarding Schools* (Minneapolis: University of Minnesota Press, 2000); S. Riess, ed., *Sports and the American Jew* (Syracuse, New York: Syracuse University Press, 1998); D. Wiggins and P. Miller, eds, *The Unlevel Playing Field: A Documentary History of the African American Experience in Sport* (Champaign, IL: University of Illinois Press, 2003); P. Vasili, *The First Black Footballer: Arthur Wharton, 1865–1930* (London: Frank Cass, 1998).

43. See, for example, J. Bale and J. Sang, *Kenyan Running: Movement Culture, Geography and Global Change* (London: Frank Cass, 1996); D. Booth and C. Tatz, *One-Eyed: A View of Australian Sport* (Sydney: Allen & Unwin, 2000); H. Beckles and B. Stoddart, eds, *Liberation Cricket: West Indies Cricket Culture* (Manchester: Manchester University Press, 1995); R. Guha, *A Corner of a Foreign Field: The Indian History of a British Sport* (London: Picador, 2002); G. Jarvie and G. Walker, eds, *Scottish Sport in the Making of a Nation: Ninety Minute Patriots* (Leicester: Leicester University Press, 1994); G. Williams, *1905 and All That: Essays on Rugby Football, Sport and Welsh Society* (Llandysul: Gomer, 1991); M. Cronin, *Sport and Nationalism in Ireland: Gaelic Games, Soccer and Irish Identity since 1870* (Dublin: Four Courts Press, 1999); M. Johnes, *A History of Sport in Wales* (Cardiff: University of Wales

Press, 2005); J. Williams, *Cricket and England: A Cultural and Social History of the Interwar Years* (London: Frank Cass, 1999); M. Polley, 'Sport and National Identity in Contemporary England', in A. Smith and D. Porter, eds, *Sport and National Identity in the Post-War World* (London: Routledge, 2004), pp. 10–30; and J. Hill and J. Williams, eds, *Sport and Identity in the North of England* (Keele: Keele University Press, 1996). Use the British Society of Sports History's on-line bibliography for an overview of these fields: http://www2.umist.ac.uk/sport/SPORTS%20HISTORY/index2.html.

44. Brailsford, op. cit. (1969).
45. Mangan, op. cit. (1981).
46. J. Tosh, *The Pursuit of History: Aims, Methods and New Directions in the Study of Modern History*, 3rd edn (London: Longman, 1999), p. 134.
47. For an accessible introduction to the issue of theory in history, see M. Fulbrook, *Historical Theory* (London: Routledge, 2002).
48. R. Holt, 'King Across the Border: Dennis Law and Scottish Football', in G. Jarvie and G. Walker, eds, *Scottish Sport in the Making of the Nation: Ninety-minute Patriots?* (Leicester: Leicester University Press, 1994), p. 363.
49. A. Marwick, *The Nature of History*, 3rd edn (Basingstoke: Macmillan, 1989), p. 142.
50. J. Horne, A. Tomlinson and G. Whannel, *Understanding Sport: An Introduction to the Sociological and Cultural Analysis of Sport* (London: Spon, 1999), p. 73.

▶ 4 Reading sports history

1. E. Dunning and K. Sheard, *Barbarians, Gentlemen and Players: A Sociological Study of the Development of Rugby Football* (Oxford: Martin Robertson, 1979); E. Dunning and K. Sheard, *Barbarians, Gentlemen and Players: A Sociological Study of the Development of Rugby Football*, 2nd edn (London: Routledge, 2004).
2. For a smaller selection of types of text, but one aimed exclusively at history students, see J. Black and D. MacRaild, *Studying History*, 2nd edn (Basingstoke: Palgrave, 2000), pp. 175–7.
3. B. Davis, J. Roscoe, D. Roscoe, and R. Bull, *Physical Education and the Study of Sport*, 5th edn (London: Mosby, 2004).
4. J. Hill, *Sport, Leisure and Culture in Twentieth-Century Britain* (Basingstoke: Palgrave, 2002).
5. Black and MacRaild, op. cit., p. 175.
6. P. Beck, *Scoring for Britain: International Football and International Politics 1900–1939* (London: Frank Cass, 1999); D. Young, *The Modern*

Olympics: A Struggle for Revival (Baltimore: Johns Hopkins University Press, 1996); G. Ryan, *The Making of New Zealand Cricket, 1832–1914* (London: Frank Cass, 2004).

7. N. Struna, 'Social History and Sport', in E. Dunning and J. Coakley, eds, *Handbook of Sports Studies* (London: SAGE, 2000), pp. 187–203; M. Polley, 'History and Sport', in B. Houlihan, ed., *Sport and Society: A Student Introduction* (London: SAGE, 2003), pp. 49–64.

8. D. Spivey, ed., *Sport in America: New Historical Perspectives* (Westport, CT: Greenwood Press, 1985); A. Smith and D. Porter, eds, *Sport and National Identity in the Post-War World* (London: Routledge, 2004).

9. T. Mason, 'Sport and Recreation', in P. Johnson, ed., *Twentieth-Century Britain: Economic, Social and Cultural Change* (London: Longman, 1994), pp. 111–26.

10. *Sociology of Sport Online*, http://physed.otago.ac.nz/sosol/home.html, accessed November 2005.

11. Amateur Athletic Foundation of Los Angeles, http://www.aafla.org/, accessed June 2005.

12. International Olympic Committee, http://www.olympic.org/uk/games/index_uk.asp, accessed August 2005; Wikipedia, http://en.wikipedia.org/wiki/Main_Page, accessed December 2005.

13. R. Cox, G. Jarvie, and W. Vamplew, eds, *Encyclopedia of British Sport* (Oxford: ABC-Clio, 2000); D. Levinson and K. Christensen, eds, *Encyclopedia of World Sport* (Santa Barbara: ABC-Clio, 1996); D. Wallechinsky, *The Complete Book of the Olympics: Athens 2004 edition* (London: Aurum Press, 2004); D. Wallechinsky, *The Complete Book of the Winter Olympics: Turin 2006 edition* (London: Aurum Press, 2006).

14. W. Vamplew, 'History', in Cox, Jarvie and Vamplew, eds, op. cit. (2000), p. 179.

15. Davis, Roscoe, Roscoe, and Bull, op. cit.

16. D. Booth, *The Field: Truth and Fiction in Sport History* (Abingdon: Routledge, 2005), p. 159.

17. John Hargeaves, *Sport, Power and Culture: A Social and Historical Analysis of Popular Sports in Britain* (Cambridge: Polity, 1986).

18. A. Guttmann, *Women's Sports: A History* (New York: Columbia University Press, 1991); P. Vertinsky, *The Eternally Wounded Woman: Women, Exercise, and Doctors in the Late Nineteenth Century* (Manchester: Manchester University Press, 1990); J. Nauright and T. Chandler, eds, *Making Men: Rugby and Masculine Identity* (London: Frank Cass, 1996); V. Burstyn, *The Rites of Man: Manhood, Politics and the Cultures of Sport* (Toronto: University of Toronto Press, 1999).

19. For an introduction to sports history and post-modernism, see M. Phillips, 'Introduction: Sport History and Postmodernism', in M. Phillips, ed., *Deconstructing Sport History: A Postmodern Analysis*

(Albany, NY: State University of New York Press, 2005), pp. 1–24; J. Hill, 'British Sports History: A Post- Modern Future?', *Journal of Sport History*, 23 (1), 1996, pp. 1–19; D. Booth, *The Field: Truth and Fiction in Sport History* (Abingdon: Routledge, 2005).
20. A. Guttmann, *The Olympics: A History of the Modern Games* (Urbana: University of Illinois Press, 1992), dust jacket.
21. Dunning and Sheard, op. cit. (1979); Dunning and Sheard, op. cit. (2004).

► 5 Primary evidence

1. D. Booth, *The Field: Truth and Fiction in Sport History* (Abingdon: Routledge, 2005), pp. 82–106.
2. A. Marwick, *The New Nature of History: Knowledge, Evidence, Language* (Basingstoke: Palgrave, 2001), pp. 166–72.
3. J. Tosh, *The Pursuit of History: Aims, Methods and New Directions in the Study of Modern History*, 3rd edn (London: Longman 1999), p. 36.
4. E.H. Carr, *What is History?* 2nd edn (Basingstoke: Palgrave, 2001), p. 18.
5. Marwick, op. cit. (2001), p. 179.
6. Ibid., p. 182.
7. Booth, op. cit., p. 86.

► 6 Primary sources in sports history 1

1. R. Cox, *History of Sport: A Guide to the Literature and Sources of Information* (Frodsham: British Society of Sports History, 1994); British Society of Sports History, 'Sports History Archives/Manuscripts', http://www2.umist.ac.uk/sport/SPORTS%20HISTORY/index2b.html, accessed November 2005.
2. J. Hill, 'Anecdotal Evidence: Sport, the Newspaper Press, and History', in M. Phillips, ed., *Deconstructing Sport History: A Postmodern Analysis* (Albany, NY: State University of New York Press, 2005), p. 118.
3. British Pathe, http://www.britishpathe.com, accessed November 2005; BBC Open News Archive, http://www.bbc.co.uk/calc/news/, accessed January 2006.
4. J. Coghlan with I. Webb, *Sport and British Politics since 1960* (Basingstoke: Falmer Press, 1990), pp. 298–9.
5. W. Vamplew, *Pay Up and Play the Game: Professional Sport in Britain, 1875–1914* (Cambridge: Cambridge University Press, 1988).
6. A. Harvey, *Football: The First Hundred Years; The Untold Story* (London: Routledge, 2005).

7. P. Lanfranchi, C. Eisenberg, T. Mason, and A. Wahl, *100 Years of Football: The FIFA Centennial Book* (London: Weidenfeld and Nicolson, 2004).

8. M. Polley, ' "The Amateur Rules": Amateurism and Professionalism in Post-War British athletics', in A. Smith and D. Porter, eds, *Amateurs and Professionals in Post-War British Sport* (London: Frank Cass, 2000), pp. 81–114.

9. T. Mason, *Association Football and English Society, 1863–1915* (Hassocks: Harvester Press, 1980), p. 6.

10. D. Smith and G. Williams, *Fields of Praise: The Official History of the Welsh Rugby Union, 1881–1981* (Cardiff: University of Wales Press, 1981); S. Bailey, *Science in the Service of Physical Education and Sport: The Story of the International Council of Sport Science and Physical Education 1956–1996* (Chichester: John Wiley, 1996); Lanfranchi, Eisenberg, Mason, and Wahl, op. cit.

11. Reproduced in Lanfranchi, Eisenberg, Mason, and Wahl, op. cit., p. 126.

12. Taken from *English Historical Documents*, vol. X, 1714–1783, pp. 533–4.

▶ 7 Primary sources in sports history 2

1. See University of Leicester, Historical Directories, http://www. historicaldirectories.org, accessed November 2005.

2. H. Salt, *Animals' Rights Considered in Relation to Social Progress* (London: George Bell, 1892); Countryside Alliance, http://www. countryside-alliance.org/, accessed November 2005.

3. R. Reno, 'Gambling and the Bible', *Florida Baptist Witness*, 13 March 2003, http://www.floridabaptistwitness.com/639.article, accessed August 2005.

4. This transcription is taken from the facsimile of the 1879 edition of Phillip Stubbes, *The Anatomie of Abuses*, which brought together the 1583, 1585, and 1595 editions. A facsimile is available at http://www.threnedlestrete.com/research/Stubbes.htm, accessed November 2005.

5. D. Storey, *This Sporting Life* (London: Longmans, 1960).

6. E.M. Forster, *A Room with a View* (Harmondsworth: Penguin, 1983); J. Betjeman, 'Pot Pourri from a Surrey Garden', in *Collected Poems*, 4th edn (London: Guild, 1980), pp. 57–8.

7. B. Malamud, *The Natural* (Harmondsworth: Penguin, 1973); P. Roth, *The Great American Novel* (Harmondsworth: Penguin, 1981).

8. P. Dickinson, ed., *Selected Poems of Henry Newbolt* (London: Hodder & Stoughton, 1981), pp. 38–9.

9. J. Hill, *Sport, Leisure and Culture in Twentieth Century Britain* (Basingstoke: Palgrave, 2002), pp. 53–7; R. Fotheringham, *Sport in Australian Drama* (Cambridge: Cambridge University Press, 1992); M. Oriard, *Dreaming of Heroes: American Sports Fiction, 1868–1980* (Chicago: Nelson-Hall, 1982).

10. 'Take Me Out to the Ball Game', Baseball Prose, Poems and Songs, on http://www.baseball-almanac.com/poetry/po_stmo.shtml, accessed November 2005.

11. J. Huntington-Whiteley (compiler), *The Book of British Sporting Heroes* (London: National Portrait Gallery, 1998).

12. Grove Art Online, http://www.groveart.com/shared/views/home. html, accessed August 2005; Mark Harden's Artchive, http://www. artchive.com/, accessed June 2005.

13. J. Germain, *In Soccer Wonderland* (London: Booth-Clibborn Editions, 1994).

14. M. Rickards, quoted in 'Welcome to the Ephemera Society', http://www.ephemera-society.org.uk/index.html, accessed January 2006.

15. R. McElroy and G. MacDougall, *Football Memorabilia: Evocative Artefacts of the Beautiful Game* (London: Carlton Books, 1999); S. Inglis, *A Load of Old Balls* (London: English Heritage, 2005); F. Slocum, *Classic Baseball Cards: The Golden Years, 1886–1956* (New York: Warner, 1987).

16. Examples include *The Times Atlas of European History*, 2nd edn (London: Times Books, 1998); J. Haywood, *The Cassell Atlas of World History* (London: Cassell, 2001).

17. For guidance on how to use maps, see P. Hindle, *Maps for the Local Historian* (London: Batsford, 1988).

18. For an exhaustive directory of historical map websites, see Perry-Castañeda Library Map Collection, University of Texas, http://www.lib. utexas.edu/maps/histus.html, accessed January 2006.

19. Held in the City of Westminster Archives Centre.

20. T. Adams with I. Ridley, *Addicted* (London: Willow, 1999).

21. L. Shackleton with D. Jack, *Clown Prince of Soccer* (London: Nicholas Kaye, 1955), p. 78.

22. H. Larwood with K. Perkins, *The Larwood Story* (1965) (Harmondsworth: Penguin, 1985), pp. 144–5.

23. The best starting point for reading about oral history is the website of the Oral History Society, which contains advice, information, resources, and links to many useful sites in the UK, the USA, and elsewhere. Oral History Society, http://www.ohs.org.uk/, accessed June 2005.

24. Society for American Baseball Research, Oral History Tapes, http://www.sabr.org/sabr.cfm?a=cms,c,351,5,178, accessed January

2006; AAFLA, Olympian Oral Histories, http://www.aafla.org/5va/ oralhistory_frmst.htm, accessed January 2006.
25. S. Caunce, *Oral History and the Local Historian* (London: Longman, 1994), p. 25.
26. M. Costa, 'An Olympian's Oral History: Aileen Riggin', Los Angeles: Amateur Athletic Foundation of Los Angeles, 2000. The full text, and many other interviews with American Olympians, is available at http://www.aafla.org.

▶ Conclusion

1. D. Booth, *The Field: Truth and Fiction in Sport History* (Abingdon: Routledge, 2005), pp. 211–6.
2. Some examples of these kind of cross-disciplinary approaches include A. Blake, *The Body Language: The Meaning of Modern Sport* (London: Lawrence and Wishart, 1996); J. Bale, 'Scientific and Romantic: The Rhetorics of the First Four-Minute Mile', *International Journal of the History of Sport*, 21 (1), 2004, pp. 118–26; J. Bale and M. Cronin, eds, *Sport and Postcolonialism* (Oxford: Berg, 2003); J. Bale, *Landscapes of Modern* Sport (Leicester: Leicester University Press, 1994); J. Wood, 'From Ashes to Dust: Who Cares About Sports Heritage?', *British Archaeology*, 85, 2005; M. Johnes and R. Mason, 'Soccer, Public History and the National Football Museum', *Sport in History*, 23 (1), 2003, pp. 115–31.
3. Some examples of work in these areas include T. Magdalinski and T. Chandler, eds, *With God on Their Side: Sport in the Service of Religion* (London: Routledge, 2002); J. Anderson, *The Soul of a Nation: A Social History of Disabled People, Physical Therapy, Rehabilitation and Sport in Britain, 1918–1970*, PhD thesis, De Montfort University, 2001; M. MacLean, 'Reading Sport in Aotearoa/New Zealand: Where's the History?', *Sporting Traditions*, 17 (2), 2001, pp. 65–71; R. Park, 'Sport and Recreation Among Chinese American Communities of the Pacific Coast from Time of Arrival to the "Quiet Decade" of the 1950s', *Journal of Sport History*, 27 (3), 2000, pp. 445–80.
4. M. Phillips, ed., *Deconstructing Sport History: A Postmodern Analysis* (Albany: State University of New York Press, 2006).
5. Booth, op. cit., p. 168.
6. See, for example, B. Southgate, *History: What and Why? Ancient, Modern, and Postmodern Perspectives* (London: Routledge, 1996); K. Jenkins, *Re-thinking History* (London: Routledge, 1991); K. Jenkins, ed., *The Postmodern History Reader* (London: Routledge, 1997).

For critiques of post-modernism as a historical approach, see A. Marwick, *The New Nature of History: Knowledge, Evidence, Language* (Basingstoke: Palgrave, 2001); R. Evans, *In Defence of History* (New York: Norton, 1999).
7. M. Phillips, 'Introduction: Sport History and Postmodernism', in Phillips, ed., op. cit., p. 7.

Further Reading and Resources

▶ Suggested reading in key areas

Early and parallel reading in a number of areas will add depth and further evidence to the themes covered in this book. In all of these cases, you must use each text's own bibliography and references to build up your own ongoing catalogue of sports history.

Large-scale histories of sport

To get depth, facts, events, and analysis, you need to read around in some histories of sport that have covered significant time spans in various countries, and sometimes larger areas. These books vary in length, but all provide a way into the development of sport over time in various settings.

D. Adair and W. Vamplew, *Sport in Australian History* (Melbourne: Oxford University Press, 1997).

W. Baker, *Sports in the Western World* (Totowa, NJ: Rowman and Little-field, 1982).

R. Cashman, *Paradise of Sport: The Rise of Organised Sport in Australia* (Melbourne: Oxford University Press, 1995).

A. Guttmann, *From Ritual to Record: The Nature of Modern Sports* (New York: Columbia University Press, 1978).

R. Holt, *Sport and the British: A Modern History* (Oxford: Oxford University Press, 1989).

C. Howell, *Blood, Sweat, and Cheers: Sport and the Making of Modern Canada* (Toronto: University of Toronto Press, 2001).

D. McComb, *Sports in World History* (London: Routledge, 2004).

J.A. Mangan and F. Hong, eds, *Sport in Asian Society: Past and Present* (London: Frank Cass, 2003).

B. Rader, *American Sports: From the Age of Folk Games to the Age of Televised Sports*, 5th edn (New York: Prentice Hall, 2003).

Historical theory and methodology

This book is designed to help you with sports history, and part of its remit is to introduce you to some wider debates about history as a discipline. However, it is beyond this book's scope to do anything more than introduce: as you will see, there is a huge literature on the nature of history, and on historians' sources and methods. You should read around in this literature, both to follow up ideas and references from this book and to help your further development as a historian and a sports historian. To help you here, I recommend the following texts. These have been written with an undergraduate history audience in mind, but are accessible to wider audience too.

M.Abbot, ed., *History Skills: A Student's Handbook* (London: Routledge, 1996).
J. Black and D.M. MacRaild, *Studying History*, 2nd edition (Basingstoke: Palgrave, 2000).
A. Marwick, *The New Nature of History: Knowledge, Evidence, Language* (Basingstoke: Palgrave, 2001).

Sport studies

This book also needs to be seen as part of the literature on the discipline and methodology of sport studies, and you can get more from it if you read it in conjunction with the following works from this growing discipline.

D. Andrews, D. Mason and M. Silk, eds, *Qualitative Methods in Sports Studies* (Oxford: Berg, 2005).
D. Booth, *The Field: Truth and Fiction in Sport History* (Abingdon: Routledge, 2005).
J. Coakley and E. Dunning, eds, *Handbook of Sports Studies* (London: Sage, 2000).
C. Gratton and I. Jones, *Research Methods for Sport Studies* (London: Routledge, 2004).
B. Houlihan, ed., *Sport and Society: A Student Introduction* (London: Sage, 2003).
J. Thomas, J. Nelson and S. Silverman, *Research Methods in Physical Activity*, 5th edition (Champaign, Illinois: Human Kinetics, 2005).

Sports history bibliographies

As you read this book, you will see that I have used many examples of books and articles about sports history throughout the text. These examples are just a tiny part of the growing literature on sports history, and you need to use specialised bibliographies to widen out the examples and, as new material is published, to add original examples and themes. The best starting point for this is the comprehensive online bibliography service provided by the British Society of Sports History (BSSH):

BSSH 'Annual Bibliographies of Publications on the History of Sport in the English Language', 'Bibliography of Publications on the History of British Sport (to 2000)', and the 'Select Bibliography of Contemporary (Primary) Publications on British Sport 1800 to 1920'. These are all available on the BSSH website at http://www2.umist.ac.uk/sport/SPORTS%20HISTORY/index2.html.

Journals and periodicals

There are numerous high-quality, peer-reviewed academic journals in sports history, and one of the best ways of reading outwards from the themes in this book is to review their back numbers and keep up to date with their new issues. The leading journals are as follows:

International Journal of the History of Sport
Journal of Olympic History*
Journal of Sport History*
Sport in History (formerly The Sports Historian)*
Sport History Review (formerly Canadian Journal for Sport History)
Sporting Traditions*

* Titles marked with an asterisk have substantial back numbers available for free on the Amateur Athletic Foundation of Los Angeles' (AAFLA) digital archive at http://www.aafla.com.

▶ Online resources

The Internet has a huge potential as a resource-base for sports historians. As well as the kind of fan- and club-based history that the Internet contains, which can be useful for information and perceptions, there are many online guides, catalogues, and databases that provide both information about sport in the past and guidance on how to locate and use different primary and secondary sources. This section provides the addresses for some of these sites that you can use to work outwards from the themes covered in this book. Remember that you need to exercise stringent quality control measures when using the Internet for research, and that you should never use the Internet as your only resource. All of the URLs given below were correct when this book went to print (August 2006). R. Cox, The Internet as a Resource for the Sports Historian (Frodsham: Sports History Publishing, 1995) remains a useful guidebook.

Timelines in sport

While this book is not a narrative history of any sport, it has made frequent reference to events from sports history. Rather than produce a timeline of these events, which would be fragmentary and limiting, you are encouraged to read around in sports history from the books and articles referenced throughout. However, there are some useful timelines available on the Internet, which you can use for quick reference to help put specific events in order. Remember that every timeline is a selective exercise, relative to the nationality, sporting, and thematic interests of its compilers.

Sports History Dates, Facts and Statistics, Chronologies, Timelines, etc. This is a collection of links to various timelines, compiled by the British Society of Sports Historians. http://www2.umist.ac.uk/sport/SPORTS%20HISTORY/index2b.html
Sports timeline, compiled by Wikipedia. http://www.answers.com/topic/sports-timeline

Sports history societies

There are active sports history societies in many countries, as well as some with international and continental remits. The following is a selection of these, which you should use to find out about current developments in the discipline, and for their many links to additional resources.

Australian Society for Sports History (ASSH). http://www.sporthistory.org/.
British Society of Sports Historians (BSSH). http://www2.umist.ac.uk/sport/SPORTS%20HISTORY/index2.html.
European Committee for Sport History (ECSH). http://www.cesh.info/.
International Society for Comparative Physical Education and Sport (ISCPES). http://www.iscpes.org/.
International Society for the History of Physical Education and Sport (ISHPES). http://www2.umist.ac.uk/sport/Sports%20History/ishpes.html.
International Society of Olympic Historians (ISOH). http://www.isoh.org/pages/index.html.
North American Society for Sport History (NASSH). http://www.nassh.org/index1.html.

Archives and record offices

By searching the catalogues of archives and record offices, you can identify thousands of primary sources for sports history. Do not just limit yourself to sport-specific collections, as plenty of material is housed in local, regional, or national collections. Here, I have given a number of national collections, and some sites, such as Access to Archives, that allow you to search across archives by keyword. Remember that if you want to use the primary sources themselves, you will still have to visit the archive in question: these links allow you to search catalogues, but not to see the sources.

Access to Archives. http://www.a2a.org.uk/.
Library and Archives Canada. http://www.collectionscanada.ca/.
National Archives (UK). http://www.nationalarchives.gov.uk/.
National Archives (USA). http://www.archives.gov/.
National Archives of Australia. http://www.naa.gov.au/.
National Archives of Ireland. http://www.nationalarchives.ie/.
National Archives of New Zealand. http://www.archives.govt.nz/.
National Archives of Scotland. http://www.nas.gov.uk/.
National Archives and Records Service of South Africa. http://www.national.archives.gov.za/.
Public Record Office of Northern Ireland. http://www.proni.gov.uk/.

Research skills

As well as the books on historical methodology referenced in the chapters, there are a number of Internet sources that can help the development of your primary research skills.

Reading, Writing, and Researching for History: A Guide for College Students
http://academic.bowdoin.edu/WritingGuides/
Internet History Sourcebooks Project
http://www.fordham.edu/halsall/
Research Methods Resources on the WWW: Historical Research Methods
http://www.slais.ubc.ca/resources/research_methods/history.htm

Miscellaneous sites

Here are some websites that will allow you to expand on specific themes from this book. Some of them appear in the References, but they are important enough to warrant special mention here.

ALTIS. This is a guide to online resources in the subject areas of hospitality, leisure, sport, and tourism. It provides searchable links to thousands of sites, including those run by academic departments, museums, halls of fame, and enthusiasts. http://altis.ac.uk/index.html.
Amateur Athletic Foundation of Los Angeles (AAFLA). Its digital archive is a peerless collection of journals, books, and reports on many aspects of sports history. http://www.aafla.org.
Arts and Humanities Data Service. This is a way into digital resources for many areas of research, including history. http://www.ahds.ac.uk.
Collect Britain. This is the British Library's collection of sounds and images on many aspects of history, including sport. http://www.collectbritain.co.uk/.
Grove Art Online. This is a searchable database of artworks that covers most of the world's major art collections. Look for artists whose work you know included sporting themes, or use sport-related search terms. http://www.groveart.com/shared/views/home.html.

Oral History Society. This contains information and guides for all aspects of oral history, and useful bibliographies and external links. http://www. ohs.org.uk/.

Perry-Castañeda Library Map Collection, University of Texas. This is an excellent collection of links to hundreds of historical maps. http://www. lib.utexas.edu/maps/map_sites/hist_sites.html.

Scholarly Sport Sites. This is a collection of links to academic sites on all aspects of the study of sport, not just its history. http://www.ucalgary. ca/lib-old/ssportsite/.

Index